THE RAGGED HEART

THE RAGGED HEART

*Selected Works From the COMPAS
Writers & Artists-in-the-Schools Program*

Edited by
Norita Dittberner-Jax

Illustrations by
Marce Wood

COMPAS
Writers & Artists-in-the-Schools
1989

Publication of this book is generously supported by the Sven and C. Emil Berglund Foundation, dedicated in memory of C. Emil Berglund.

COMPAS programs are made possible in part by grants provided by the Minnesota State Arts Board, through an appropriation by the Minnesota State Legislature. The Minnesota State Arts Board received additional funds to support this activity from the National Endowment for the Arts. COMPAS is the recipient of a McKnight Foundation Award administered by the Minnesota State Arts Board, and is a member of United Arts. In the past year, the COMPAS Writers & Artists-in-the-Schools program has received generous support from the Hugh J. Anderson Foundation, the Ashland Oil Foundation, the Cargill Foundation, Fingerhut Corporation, the Jostens Foundation and Land O'Lakes.

As always, we are grateful for the hundreds of excellent teachers throughout Minnesota who sponsor COMPAS Writers & Artists-in-the-Schools residencies. Without their support and hard work, the writers and artists would not weave their magic, and the student work we celebrate in this book would not spring to life.

ISBN 0-927663-14-7

COMPAS
305 Landmark Center
75 West Fifth Street
St. Paul, Minnesota 55102

Molly LaBerge, Executive Director
Randolph Jennings, Director, Arts Education Programs

TABLE OF CONTENTS

2. OUR OWN LIVES

3. SELF-PORTRAITS AND PORTRAITS

4. DREAMS AND IMAGINATION

5. STORIES

6. NATURE

7. THE WORLD

INTRODUCTION

The appearance of the annual COMPAS anthology is always cause for celebration. The publication of *The Ragged Heart*, this year's volume like its predecessors, marks the end of a year of intense, imaginative activity by students and writers involved in the Writers & Artists-in-the-Schools program. Its appearance is a way of recognizing the risk students take when they engage in the process of making art.

As the editor of this year's edition, I spent the warm weeks of the summer reading the work of hundreds of student writers. Far from being repetitive, reading the poems and prose pieces filled the days with clear images and foot-tapping rhythms (try chopping the celery to "we were born with the milk inside us, we were born with sturdy bones"). See what I mean? The only pain involved arose out of the need to choose among so many strong stories and poems.

What these student writers bring to their work is the gift of themselves, their lives, their experience, their imagination. That is the raw material that we all begin with. It is the only place to start. The visiting writer helps them shape that material, calls it forth, really, establishes an atmosphere in which that material can be safely articulated. I come away from editing this anthology delighted by the work of the students.

I am also moved by the contribution of my colleagues. As editor, I can get an overview of the program, something I cannot do as a program writer. I have found it really exciting to see the work as a whole, what writers evoke and what students can write when they are in the particular atmosphere of playfulness that working artists establish.

Teaching writing to students is intense. Program writers have to work fast. For many of us, the residency begins late Sunday afternoon or evening, when we arrive in town, a stranger, looking for the motel and the cafe; on Monday morning, finding the schedule, the school, the class, the students. Monday, Tuesday, Wednesday, Thursday, Friday, a week full of helloes and good-byes. By the time we leave Friday afternoon, our bags are full of poems and stories that existed only as an idea, an image, five days earlier. We hope we leave behind students that are happy with themselves for the work they have accomplished. We hope we leave behind a few who are "hooked," who will turn to writing on their own, spontaneously, because it is a pleasurable thing to do.

We hope that sometime in the years to come, if not now, that a memory will remain of an afternoon in school when the assignments and book reports fell away, and pencils moved swiftly across the page propelled by an internal rhythm all its own.

I think you can hear that kind of rhythm in the pieces included in *The Ragged Heart*. I chose them for their strength and freshness, for the range of their concerns, and for their direct access to the heart. I hope the volume will be useful and easy to teach from. I don't know a better way to teach than to use strong examples from students themselves. One good example is worth countless explanations about how to do it.

To the students and their families, I hope this book will appear on hundreds of coffee tables of parents, grandparents, godparents, aunts, uncles, and cousins. I hope you have shameless pride in what you have written and the humility to write again.

Have your picture taken too. Congratulations. Well-done. Bravo.

Norita Dittberner-Jax
August, 1989

We were born with milk inside us
We were born with the flying crows
We were born with the house creaking
We were born with sturdy bones

We were born with the snowflakes falling
We were born with the whistling birds
We were born with the wind blowing
We were born with our own deep breath

Group Poem after a song by Sarah Pirtle :: Kindergarten
Webster Magnet Elementary School :: St. Paul

Listen child:
Hear that?
It's the wind blowin' through your life
It's leaving crumpled leaves
for you to pick up, and
dirt and dust for you to
sweep away.

Listen child:
Hear that?
It's God, he's reaching out his hand.
He's letting you grab hold and
Come with him. Go, I say.

Listen child:
Hear that?
It's the snow, falling on you like your baby blanket.
Go under it, I say, it will hold you safely.

Listen child:
Hear that?
It's traffic, trying to confuse you,
Leave it be, I say, and take a side street.

Listen child:
Hear that?
It's my heart tellin' me
I love you.

Sarah Russell :: Grade 6
Webster Magnet School :: St. Paul

In my picture, my mom is doing an impression of Elvis Presley. My friend, Jessica, is over, wondering what the heck she's doing. I am 10 years old, and already thinking I'm going to commit suicide! What a moron! The air is clean and it's a sunny day out. My mom has the song "Hound Dog" on full blast and she's singing at the top of her lungs. She's standing on top of a green chair, doing Chubby Checker's version of "The Twist." After I leave, I can hear her singing and panting because she's getting tired. After the song is over, I notice she's recorded it, because she plays it 15 times after that. And at the end of each song, she yells, "Yeaaaaaay!" I wonder if she's eating Kellogg's Product 19.

Amber Dryden :: Grade 5
Crestview Elementary School :: Cottage Grove

Hen Pecked!

Chicken, chicken, in my belly,
Cluck disgust — I need to yelly.

Sister's feet are on the T.V.
Peck her toenails just for me.

Mom has not washed my socks,
Think I'll give her chicken pox.

Dad cleans goop out of his ear,
Using Mom's good pen to clear.

Chicken, chicken, lay an egg,
Chicken, chicken, on his leg.

Andi Sandven :: Grade 6
Avon Elementary School :: Avon

My mom was mad. I went too far. I had to clean the house. I had to rake the leaves. I went to bed at 4:00. My brother got a popsicle. I rode my bike. Then I got a spanking. I had to start all over again. I had to clean the house again. I had to rake the leaves again and go to bed at 3:00. My brother got another popsicle. "Go to bed at 2:00." I'm cleaning again.

Cheryl Weirauch :: Grade 2
Valley View Elementary School :: Columbia Heights

MY DAD

My dad sits on the bucket milking our
cows until we get our parlor
set up. His bald head rests against
the cows's body. Sometimes he squirts
me. When he is done, he walks
really fast to the house, tall
with his boots on, and puts the milk
in the pasturizer. Then he gives the rest
to the cats. We laugh a lot.
I am thankful he gives us milk
even though I don't like it.

Jennifer Smith :: Grade 5
Kerkhoven-Murdock Elementary School :: Kerkhoven

MY DAD

My dad sits in the living room
with his good thoughts in his mind
I see my dad working outside
like a slave in a mine.
His body is strong as a wrestler's
his face has honest looks like
a puppy.
He thinks of me as a bright
intelligent girl beside him.
I would give him love
until he dies.
I'll put the sun over his head.
As his beard grows grey
good memories will nest in his
beard forever.
As his body stands on the earth
he feels loved like a rose.
When he feels let down, there's always
somebody to shine over him.

Colette Tauer :: Grade 6
Lino Lakes Elementary School :: Lino Lakes

As far as people go, I am not one who cares about family history. It's just too painful for me. Both of my parents died when I was three years old. Being reminded of them hurt. So when I was moved from my home (my parents' home) on the East Coast to my grandmother's home on the West Coast nine years ago, it took me away from the memories. Since I had no brothers or sisters, there was nothing left to remind me of them, or so I thought.

When I came home from school one day, I saw a huge mess in the living room. All of a sudden my grandma came bustling into the room. Even though my grandpa had died five years ago, grandma didn't stop being the energetic, friendly, loving lady she had always been. So when my silver-haired grandma came into the room, I was happy to see her, despite the living room.

"Welcome," my grandma said, and laughed. "It's spring cleaning."

I gave a little groan. Ever since I came into this house, I showed a dislike for cleaning. My grandma, knowing this, with a twinkle in her blue eyes, said I could skip this day of spring cleaning. So before she changed her mind, I bounded up the stairs, taking two at a time. Suddenly, I stopped. I was on the second to the last step. Blocking my way at the top of the stairs was a gigantic cherry wood chest with a label that said: PROPERTY OF MR. AND MRS. JOSEPH RAMSEY, otherwise known as my parents.

I felt like running back down the stairs, away from that chest, those memories. But for the first time in a long time, curiosity overcame me, and I advanced to the chest.

Slowly I pushed it back a little ways. I then unlatched the chest with shaky fingers. My mind was spinning. Questions floated through my head. "What's in there? Where did it come from, and why is it here?" were only some of the many. I slowly pulled the lid up. There was a musty smell to the chest. It almost made me reel back. I would of, except for a huge marriage certificate, encased in glass, that was dated 1898. The couple was my great-grandparents. My curiosity, aroused again, made me dig deeper into the chest . . . .

About two hours later I was half way down the chest. Surrounding me were photo albums, yearbooks, various school awards, and even diplomas. Suddenly I stopped rummaging through the chest. What was I doing? I was reminding myself of my past. Yet I wasn't crying. Suddenly I heard a noise on the stairs.

I looked down and saw my grandmother at the bottom of the stairs. She said not a word, but looked at me and gave me a slight smile. I smiled back and turned back to the cherry wood chest. A gold picture frame caught my eye. I picked it out of the chest, dusted it off and saw Mom, Dad and myself looking at the camera. Tears of joy streamed down my face. The people I never wanted to find out about were suddenly looking up at me, as my parents, smiling. I then realized that there is nothing that will ever make me forget them, and I don't want to forget about them anymore.

Katie Murphy :: Grade 6
Caledonia Elementary School :: Caledonia

You are tacks on the ground
on rainy days, but when
the sun shines on you,
you just want to play
and be happy.
As soon as you are sad,
the rain comes,
your rage that the sun left
is stronger than before,
you turn into pins and needles.
The pain of your burden
weighs me down,
and I long for the sun.

David Korus :: Grade 3
Southview Elementary School :: Apple Valley

She used to wake me up and tickle my feet.

I told her not to pull off the covers
but I didn't mean for her to go away.

We put on towels and sang old choir hymns
but maybe my voice was too shrill.

During dinner we let spaghetti
strings hang out of our mouths.

Mom and Dad told us to stop and all too soon
she agreed.

Soon she was the one who slept late.

When I tickled her feet she
groaned and yelled at me.

I tried to be like her but I couldn't catch up.

Then she was gone for a long time.
When she came back her face
looked older and her eyes sagged.

I just couldn't catch up.

Ann Marie Healey ::
Benilde-St. Margaret's High School :: Plymouth

I Want to Speak

I want to speak for my brother
who gets hurt very much.
I want to speak for those needles
that poke him one by one.
I want to speak for those tears
that roll down his cheeks.
I want to speak for that tumor
that hurts my brother very much.
I want to speak for those doctors and nurses
that are taking good care of him.
I want to speak for my mom who tried to help him.
I want my brother to get better.

Frankie Bergeson :: Grade 5
Washington Elementary School :: Rochester

My brother enters a world
        of harmony when the
        moon overrides the sun
His frailness and sickness
        will terminate till the
        winds stop caressing the
        earth.
I see him engulfed in a
        heaven of radiation
        the color of youth returning
        to his peaked cheeks.
The only traces of his past
        becomes a dim shadow and
        a bent baseball card on the
        floor.

Melissa Sundeen :: Grade 8
Oltman Junior High School :: St. Paul Park

The spirit of this place lives in a house,
a place with lots of memories.
In the beginning when the house was made
it had memories of a happy family,
a family that once lived there.
And, after many years
it had memories of an unhappy family
that consisted of a mother, a father,
and two children.
One summer there were lots of fights.
And now only a man
and a little black dog named Spunky
live there.

Jolene Johnson :: Grade 5
Tanglen Elementary School :: Minnetonka

Finally the day had come, now I must finish the business I had put off since my father's death. "The cabin must be sold," I kept telling myself, but how could I part with something that my father had loved with all his heart? My mind was jumbled with such thoughts as I packed my tote bag with lunch, a flashlight, and a key to unlock the cage out back.

It has been a hard few months. I've been trying to put my life back together, but I just can't let go of the anger I have over my dad's death. He was so young and full of life, but I don't understand why I feel so cheated when it is really him who was cheated out of a long, happy life. Even though I know dying put him out of his misery, I just wish we could have had a little more time together. There are so many questions left unanswered, especially his reasons for not telling me he had been slowly dying from heart disease for several years.

As I stepped outside to my waiting car, I realized that the weather reflected my feelings. It was cold, grey, and windy — snow was in the forecast so I hoped to reach my destination before the weather became too threatening.

When I got to the winding road that leads to the cabin, I realized this would be the last time to travel it. The car slowed to a stop near the front door. As I got out I stopped at the old oak tree. It seemed like just yesterday I was there with dad. I'll never forget the day he hung the swing almost 10 years ago. As I looked up I noticed the strong limbs of the tree, they reminded me so much of father, big, strong, and powerful. Softly, I whispered, "Why did he have to go, we all need him for so many things." The tree seemed to understand me and as the wind blew it protected me just like dad would have.

Now as I moved to the door I could feel a strange presence, it was almost as though my dad was there with me. When I went inside everything was a reminder to me of what it used to be like, the days we spent out in the woods observing the beauty surrounding the area. I walked around the room collecting the last few items I needed. And then my eyes fell upon a picture. In the photo was myself and my father out on the back porch. We were both so happy then.

I sat down in his favorite chair and looked out the large bay window. Snow was beginning to fall and the animals seemed to have disappeared. Dad really loved it here; it's too bad I must sell this place. I know Dad would have wanted to be here for the last few days of his life, instead of in that hospital. Now my thoughts began to wander. "Why did it have to be my father? I loved him so much!" Then I finally let go of my anger and all those unshed tears rolled down my cheeks.

After a couple of hours, I realized it was getting late, so I packed my belongings and locked the door for the last time, it felt like I was shutting a chapter in my life. Then I headed around back to finish my last chore. It took a while, but after a lot of digging around in my purse, I came up with a key. Then I moved toward the cage. Inside was a big, black hawk. This had been one of the last projects I worked on with him. "Blackie" had fallen from a nest when he was a baby. Together we nursed him back to health. Dad really enjoyed doing that, but now it was time to let him go. I knelt down, "Blackie, I can't take care of you any longer; it's time for you to be free. Good-bye, you've been a good friend, I wish you good luck!" As he looked at me I could read the words in his eyes. He ap-preciated the help we had given him. I unlocked the door and gave him a boost that sent him soaring into the air. Soon he flew away and at last I could say, "Good-bye Daddy."

AnnMarie Stroshane :: Grade 10
Richfield Senior High School :: Richfield

Manuel tried to focus his eyes on the shifting beach before him. The tiny crabs tumbling over the rocks were so flawlessly camouflaged that the entire scene appeared as an optical illusion created by God.

Manuel blinked hard. He could still see the picture reflected on the backs of his eyelids. As his eyes slowly opened their gaze rested on his naked feet.

Through the years he had learned to mimic his mother almost perfectly. "Manuel—he going to have big hands and feet like his papa." Like his papa . . . .

He pinched his eyelids together hard until he could be sure that the flood of tears would not flow from the swelling ducts. His mama had told him many times that crying would not bring back his papa. But sometimes at night, when the moon shone brightly through his window, Manuel thought he could hear his mama crying.

An icy wind brought the skinny boy's thoughts back to the beach. He shuddered and turned his face toward the blistering sun. Manuel had once asked how the sun could be so scorching and yet the wind could burn his lungs. Someone had told him, "The winds from the ocean come from a place where the sun does not shine."

Manuel tried to imagine such a horrible place. "No trees," he thought, "no animals, no brilliant blue sky. A place where people wandered lost and cold forever." He could understand why the wind would want to leave a place like that.

He once had written a story about the place where the winds come from. Manuel had never felt so frightened in all of his life. The other children had laughed at him because his face had glowed hot and his tongue had become painted to the roof of his mouth so that no words would come out.

Manuel hated school. He hated the children who laughed at him and pointed their dirty fingers at his brown skin. Every day, as soon as the last bell echoed its final chorus of the school day, Manuel ran home as fast as he could. Then, after all of his chores were done, he would point his little bike in the direction of the beach. There, perched on his rock, he would watch the dolphins propel themselves out of the water, then plummet back down again creating a tremendous splash.

But most of the time Manuel sat waiting for his papa to come home. He knew that one day a white dot where the lavender sky meets the dark waters would grow into a gallant vessel with proud white sails and pink-faced sailors laughing and dancing. And one of those sailors would be his papa.

Manuel closed his eyes again and imagined a speck on the horizon growing larger and larger. Then the speck became the sun glimmering off the back of a gray dolphin. The dolphin was coming straight toward the shore. It raced past the spot where the other dolphins were playing. It appeared to be headed directly toward Manuel.

Manuel flinched as if someone had suddenly flicked their fingers very near his eyes. The dolphin stopped.

It was staring at Manual.

Manuel stared back.

(to be continued)

Shannon Williams :: Grade 12
Long Prairie High School :: Long Prairie

Calvin Lives in Turkey. He has spikey black hair. He's pretty tall, has blue eyes and always wears a black shirt. Some people are constantly saying, "Get out of here." Other people say that he's funny. Calvin's interests are mainly nothing. He never wants to do anything. He's real lazy, very clumsy and never listens. He walks lazy, not like his brother Lou.

The reason Calvin doesn't live in the same house as Lou is because Lou doesn't want him to. Calvin is fifteen years old and is in the seventh grade. His teacher is not the happiest teacher now that Calvin is in her class. She said she would rather have Lou any day. Every one else thinks the same. He's very popular but it's because he's bad. Otherwise people don't really like him.

Lou Diamond Phillip lives in Tokyo. He has yellow hair and very tiny black eyes and always wears a yellow shirt. Most people say that he's nice. Some other people say, "You're not like your brother, Calvin." Lou's interests are everything. He likes writing, playing sports, math, etc. Lou is very smart, nice and generous, a good listener and active. He walks normally, not like his brother Calvin.

Lou knows many kids and they know him. He's very popular, but not because he's bad. He's very nice. Once upon a time Lou was going to the store and he bumped into his brother Calvin. Lou asked Calvin what he was doing in Tokyo. Calvin said, "There was a tornado and it terminated my house. It was a terrible sight."

"Do you mean you watched it?" said Lou.

"Yes, I stood right outside and watched it."

"Good grief," said Lou. There was a silence . . . . . Finally Lou said, "Well you're going to have to live with me for a while."

"Yeah!" said Calvin.

The next few weeks were a disaster. Calvin, instead of being boring and quiet, decided to be loud and annoying. He nearly wrecked the house.

Then Lou got so annoyed he walked up to Calvin and said, "Stop ruining my house."

Calvin said, "Look at my bedroom," as if he didn't hear a word. Then Lou fainted. For about three hours Lou was sleeping. When Lou woke up, hoping Calvin was gone, he looked at Calvin's bedroom. Calvin was still there.

Later that night Lou was watching the news. He saw Calvin's city. And he was shocked. Not one little speck of wood was on the ground. Then Lou decided to do something to Calvin. That night Lou painted red dots all over Calvin. The next morning when he woke up Calvin found himself bombarded with red dots. When he went to show Lou, Lou said, "You'll have to go back to Turkey."

Calvin said, "I can't because there was a tornado."

Lou said, "Not any more! The news said so." So Calvin left. From that time on Lou was the happiest man on earth.

Brian Vossen :: Grade 3
Centennial Elementary School :: Richfield

(Curtain opens on James' house. James is pretending to play heavy metal guitar, digging out completely on the music. He sings to himself Joan Jett's song "I Love You So Much It Hurts." James' mother is on the other side of the stage cutting the hair of Mrs. Johnson, the next door neighbor.)

Mother: I don't know what to do about James. His grades aren't good. How are your kids doing?

Mrs. Johnson: Oh, my kids are doing great. They all get straight A's. And they sure don't act like that.

(James is completely lost in his music, dancing around in jerks and jumps.)

Mother: James! James! Settle down.

(He does, for a brief moment.)

Mother: James, how does this look?

(James walks over calmly, inspects Mrs. Johnson's haircut.)

James: Looks fine. Looks just fine.

(James goes calmly behind Mom. When she cannot see him, he suddenly makes a broad, violent gesture towards her. He suddenly acts calm again, goes back to his music.)

Mrs. Johnson: Does he always act like that?

Mother: James! Settle down.

Mrs. Johnson: How is your cat, Buttons?

Mother: Oh, he's fine.

Mrs. Johnson: He's a good cat. He's nice and sweet. Not like your son.

Mother: James!

(James pretends to calm down.)

Mother: Well, Mrs. Johnson, how does this look?

Mrs. Johnson: That looks fine. Thanks.

(Mrs. Johnson exits. James comes over, picks up some of the hair clippings, and throws them around.)

Mother: James, stop that. Pick up this hair.

(James picks up some more, throws it around the room. Mother comes over to him and slaps him.)

Mother: Now pick up all this hair and put it in a bag. Do it now before Buttons swallows it.

(She exists. James looks at Buttons. He picks up the bag. He looks at Buttons some more. He goes to a drawer and pulls out a knife.)

James: Here, Buttons.

Group Play
Worthington Area Junior High School :: Worthington

Gray is the sound of a thunderstorms' rustle
or stair creaking.
It's pencil lead tapping on the sheet of paper.
It's the sound of a cold attic.
Gray is the feeling of being sick for a long, long, time
or having someone special die.
It reminds me of the time I lost my dog, and my great grandpa.
Gray in my mouth is cold mushroom soup and cavities.
Someday gray will become the color of my hair.

Group Poem :: Grade 2
Katherine Curren Elementary School :: Hopkins

WHERE DID YOU GO?

Where did you go? The doctors said
that you would be fine and that you could
go home and that your heart attack was fine.
I stayed with you as long as I could
but I had to go to school. Why did I
have to find you? My heart crumbled, my
throat got dry, I felt so sorry for you, just
lying there stiff. Was it my fault I wasn't
there to call 911? Do you still love me
after what happened? Do you?

Andy Duffy :: Grade 8
Central Middle School :: Columbia Heights

He could organize the rope on my shoe,
he knew a bear's print from a deer's,
he transformed our bunk bed into
a teepee, a battleship, a mansion.

Then the scary man in blue and badge
with a walkie-talkie to bridge the void
to brother's white room.

The cold long ebony box bed
with the cover open, brother sleeping
The innocent questions:
"Where's Mike? When will he be home?"
The careful caring answers: "He's happy now."

When hideous monsters surround my bed
in the middle of the night,

The glow in the dark ball.

Jim Hawkins :: Grade 12
Cretin-Derham Hall :: St. Paul

Spying

Here I am on the top of my stairs, listening to the blaring music and seeing the walls and the floor underneath my uncle's moving feet as the sun shines outside. I hear the humming coming from my uncle's mouth as he rocks to the music, twisting and jumping up and down in his faded jeans and a Harley T-shirt. My mom and dad are sitting upstairs watching the latest Cosby Show episode. Soon they notice I'm gone. My parents yell for me. "Kimmy, where are you? Come out from where you are hiding." My uncle also yells for me. "Hey, turkey, where are you?" I am trapped. I have been caught spying on my uncle. There is no escape. All I can do is laugh, just like my uncle, my mom, and my dad all do, as they realize where I am. Soon grabbing the railing, I scramble to my feet, slipping on the green carpeted steps, trying to avoid the arms reaching out to tickle-torture me. Of course, I'm not fast enough, but I don't mind. And then I see my uncle's smiling face—the one that is now only a memory.

Kim Wayne :: Grade 8
Central Middle School :: Columbia Heights

I had been playing on the beach when I looked up and saw a door. Supper was about ready and my mother was calling me to come inside. I was curious as to what was behind the door, so I did not pay any attention to her.

This door had been around a while. Strips of wood peeled off and the crumbling, bitterly colored brown paint flaked to the touch. The design was simple. Just two squares symmetrically placed on each side. The door knob was old and tarnished. When new it must have been shiny and smooth. Now the copper plating was brown and tarnished, even coming completely off in some places. The hinges were rusty and stiff. You could tell that it squeaked and creaked because the red rust rested undisturbed in the joints.

I looked down in the sand and saw a flicker of reflected light. It was as small as a grain of sand but it was different. It shimmered in the light like something of a golden color. As I bent down to pick it up I could feel my stomach churn, knees lock, and hands shake in hope that it might be a coin of times past or even just a jewel that had been recently lost. I picked whatever it was up and felt something smooth with notches cut in the side and grooves that were narrow and shallow but long. My eyes were closed tightly with wishes, but I could feel that it was a key. There was an ornate dragon with emerald eyes staring up at me when I had opened mine. Rubies gleamed with fury to form fire coming from the golden head.

I was about to open the door when I thought of the last time my curiosity had tricked me. It had been another door in my family's new home. I thought there was a closet lurking behind the door. It seemed most certain that that was what it would be, but I opened the door and there was a bathroom. That is what my life has been like, full of surprises and many disappointments. Who knows what the other side of the door would hold, but it would either be a surprise or disappointment. One other problem I had was that I always felt guilty when I did something I was not sure of.

My mind was made up. I would open the door just to find out what was on the other side. The door wouldn't move. Of course, it was locked and I had to put the key in. I tried again but it only moved about an inch. It was the hinges as I had thought before. After jiggling, pushing, and kicking with all of my might it finally opened about a foot. It still was not enough for me to squeeze my way into, but I was now able to push my way inside.

When I looked around I saw nothing but white. It was one big cloud, fluffy, light, and airy. One of the first things I noticed was that the weight had lessened at my feet. In fact, I even thought I felt myself rising. I couldn't tell because the clouds, or whatever that white stuff was, was swirling around me. I couldn't see the door anymore because it was covered by the clouds. I was lost. I had no idea if I would ever get home again or even find anyplace.

It felt like I had been there for hours though I really had no sense of time. I found the edge of those monsterous clouds after having moved about a hundred feet. I saw lush green grass and I could hear birds singing. There were trees of all sort blowing in the wind and flowers of every color of the rainbow. A stream was crackling, gurgling, and it almost seemed like home, but it wasn't.

The only reason why I knew it wasn't just a meadow on earth was because it was too perfect. There was even a house that looked like mine and I thought I saw my mother. My little brother, who always seems to be fighting, was quiet and peaceful. There was no garbage on the ground to mar the scene. There was nothing wrong, including no problems.

When my father came home from work I ran to greet him. I had never done that before. I tried speaking but they could not hear me. I did not know what to do. It was almost as if I was a ghost and my body was still living.

A butterfly that flew by was singing. "What," I said. "Butterflies don't sing."

"They do here," said a voice from above. The voice was sweet and soft, almost like a bird. I tried fervently to see who it was. I could see nothing but the animals around.

"Who said that?" I called. "I can't see you anywhere."

"I am Moose Goof. You must not be from around here because everyone has seen me before," said the voice again.

"You are right. I am not from around here," I said. I am trying to find my way back home, but I do not know if that is possible."

"It is possible but not easy," said Moose Goof. "You must first find the dragon. He is the ruler here and will decide if you are allowed back. If not you'll have to stay."

"But how does he decide who will be allowed to leave."

"If you are helpful and friendly to everyone here, he will let you do as you please."

"I have only one more question before I leave. How do I find the dragon?"

"I will show you the way if you will get me some water. That's one thing a cloud needs a lot of."

I found a hose and gave Moose some water. He showed me the way by air until we came to a clearing. There I was set down and told that I had to go on by myself. I found a very small castle about the size of a doll house. In it was a small dragon just about like the one on the key but real and moving.

I asked him if I would be allowed to leave. He said that I could only go if I came back every week to make sure the clouds had water. (You see, Moose Goof was his best friend.)

In eagerness to get home, I hastily agreed. He showed me the edge where I had entered and led me through the clouds with his emerald eyes. We came to the door and I said good-bye.

I found myself on the sand again with the waves gently crashing into the shore. I walked home to supper that evening only to return every week. I grew to like that. I was able to think more deeply than before and know myself better. Moose Goof is gone now but for a while he was my best friend. I do miss that place now, but it was all for the best.

Mindi Rylander :: Grade 8
Plymouth Middle School :: Plymouth

I guess the clearest thing I can remember that involved me and my grandparents is the summer I was 12. Every year my brother and I would go to their big farm where peace seemed to just rest on our shoulders. It was so beautiful, so refreshing the way it felt in the morning to wake up smelling the blueberry muffins that grandmother was preparing especially for me and my brother. I could just stay there in bed and listen to the old radio talking about the current price of hogs in Iowa. The sound of the radio voices was low but the feeling of peace was there when I looked into the white painted fence containing the cattle of the year for grandpa. It was the first time I can remember actually feeling the whole world was mine and that I was one of the luckiest persons to have such a great pair of people guiding my life.

One hot August day my brother and grandpa set out to do the daily chores and start baling the hay. I always wanted to be able to bale the hay with the "men" but all I seemed to be able to do was "make the men lunch." I don't know, I guess I wanted to be able to be treated like everyone else. I suppose I decided to take that day as my opportunity. I dressed myself in grandpa's old blue and white striped overalls and Funks cap and started down the land to the field. It was a big field and it seemed to take forever to get there but I suppose that was when time seemed like forever and forever was way too long for me.

I waited and waited in the hot sun for my brother, grandpa and grandma to make another round and pick me up on their old, rickety cart. Well, they passed again and picked me up and off to work I went. I pulled the big bales with all my might and threw them onto the nicely straight rows. The smell of the hay was so crisp and clean I thought my whole world had opened up through a door I had never touched or even seen. I tried my hardest to keep up with my grandpa. He seemed to run circles around me and I felt like I was beginning to "get in the way." For some reason I have a feeling that my grandpa had known I was "in the way" for a lot longer than I could imagine.

As the cart became smaller and smaller the room got less and less and my grandpa and brother madder and madder. I wasn't sure if I would be able to have any more fun. My grandpa made a suggestion of me climbing to the top of the bales and just sitting there until we pulled the cart into the big red barn where he stored the hay for the seasons to come. I hoisted myself to the top which took a lot of my energy and sat there in the hot, sticky sun. I didn't understand how the beautiful fresh-smelling air could turn into hot and sticky air. A little time passed and my brother climbed on top with me and we just sat there trying to catch our breath. I couldn't believe he was so tired, but now I realize maybe the 30 bales of hay to my two was a little different. The day had seemed so long and tiring I couldn't believe we had done so much. We pulled the tractor out of the field and put the cart in the old big barn.

Kristi Harris :: Grade 9
East Senior High School :: Mankato

GRANDMA

She is like silk waving
in the air
waiting for the day
she is lifted up to
heaven in the chariot.
Her heart beats faster
and swift like water
splashing on the beach
when she thinks about
the lost love.
She makes dolls that
seem to come alive
with the touch of her hand.

Shaun Karson :: Grade 6
Bemidji Middle School :: Bemidji

My grandmother's name is an old fashioned
dance. She is waltzing in her finest
clothes, a pink silk dress drenched
with lace. She feels like a dove
in the blue sky and can't stop,
not even if she tried. I told her it's time
to go, but she stayed and danced and danced.
I screamed my heart out, but still
she stayed dancing. I told her
it was midnight. She stopped and thought
about what she was doing,
and she walked out the door, leaving me.

Erica Hertz :: Grade 5
Sunset Hill Elementary School :: Wayzata

Childhood is like a yo yo.
When it is at the bottom, you are a baby.
People pinch your cheeks.
When it is at the middle, you are six years old.
When it is almost to the top, you are a teenager.
You get to be more mature.
Now you are at the top, you are a grownup.
You have to pay taxes.
Oh no! I just got my electric bill. It says,
You pay 500 dollars today!
You want your Mommy and Daddy! Help!

Roy Fisher :: Grade 2
Solway Elementary School :: Bemidji

Childhood is a caterpillar.
Thunderclap! Roll into a ball
and hide, a leaf your covert abode.

The human children
fascinated by your cuteness—
but then a ripple, a burst, what now?
So exciting, yet frightening.
You are changing, you know it.
Will it hurt? How long will it take?
So many questions for such finite minds.

Slowly you melt. All your thoughts,
every figment of the past, melting.

You are free! Such clumsiness
with these new wings.
Remember what you saw through child's eyes.

Those beautiful creatures soaring—
How I wish one of them would show me how.
But I must do it alone. I wait for courage to peak.
Then, I leap from childhood
and know the majesty of the butterfly.

Sarah Haiden :: Grade 8
Presentation of Mary School :: Maplewood

FIRST CONFESSION

I walk to the front
of the huge holy house,
my footsteps echoing
click, click, click,
my peers behind me,
eyes huge.
I pass the empty pews
old and worn,

I enter the small
room of dull colors
where the man
in the white robe
puts his hand on my head
as I sputter and sweat
out my first confession.

Four Hail Marys.
A piece of cake.

Tracee O'Brien :: Grade 8
Central Middle School :: Columbia Heights

ME AT TWO

Seven years ago when I was two
and my brother Chad was five
I wanted to ride the school bus.
One day I went to the bus stop
with my brother and the bus driver
brought me around the neighborhood.
Then my brother and his friends
Tom and Kelly put me
between them and I walked
into kindergarten with my brother.
His teacher was going to call my mom.
My brother said, "Go home
with Mommy," and I yelled
"I stay."

Jason Klosterbuer :: Grade 5
West Elementary School :: Worthington

In third grade at Parkway Elementary I ALMOST got married to N.M. I was going to marry him on the playground after lunch. I had bridesmaids, a flower girl, and my friend was pretending to be my mother-in-law. Me and N.M. were getting married on a swingset. I was wearing my First Communion dress because it was my best and favorite dress. We were almost married, when the whistle blew and we had to go in. Me and N.M. got in a fight that afternoon, so we never got married.

Shawna Giese :: Grade 5
Parkway Elementary School :: St. Paul

Here's to you, you hard-back, literal pain-in-the-rear, you pencil-thrower, confusion wrought, putrid, shapeshifter of thousands of uncomfortable shapes.

Here's to you, you back-breaking, hip-wrenching creature of class. With your wire mesh confines, you entrap legs and wreak havoc on knees.

Here's to you, you gum-striken, graffiti-scrawled, cage of conflicts. Now that I'm gone, may you not rest in peace, but rather in pieces.

Debbie Gonnella :: Grade 12
John Marshall Senior High School :: Rochester

You look at a clock as if it were
alive. You watch the hands
move slowly around like children
on a merry-go-round. You watch
as time goes by; the seconds
go by fast, the hours
go by slow. You watch,
waiting, like a cat
ready to pounce. The seconds go
fast, the hours go slow
like cars in a traffic jam,
cars in rush hour.
When you watch time you
look back at all the time
you've wasted not watching.

Jamie Hemmila :: Grade 8
McGregor High School :: McGregor

Farewell

Good bye, good bye, don't cry
You might be sad, Good bye
Good bye, Good bye, don't cry

Good bye old desk
that held our stuff.
Good bye books, good bye hooks.
Good bye chalkboards
names and checks.
Good bye, Good bye, don't dry

Good bye kitchen
that baked the bood
pizzas, tacos, dunkers all
Good bye tickets, POW awards
Good bye stars
teachers smiles
Good bye, Good bye, don't cry

Good bye swings
that took me up
to tree top tall
Good bye strong walls
that held up 50 years
Good bye Mr. Moore who kept it clean
Good bye Mrs. Soloman who cooks and laughs
Good bye, Good bye, don't cry.

Good bye old school of leaks and cracks
    and 50 years of children's tears
Good bye to all the muddy tracks
    and hallway birthday cheers.
Good bye, Good bye, don't cry.

Group Poem :: Grade 2
Wyoming Elementary School :: Wyoming

Note: The Wyoming Elementary School was closed at the end of the
    1988–89 school year.

If I could daydream in school
I'd pull the fire alarm
I'd run through the halls
Throw bread in the lunchroom
Be very bad and get detention
Get kicked out of school
I'd like to be a bad boy for once
That's a day I'd never forget.

Donald Warner :: Grade 4
Wyoming Elementary School :: Wyoming

First you fold it,
Then you sneak around,
Wait until she is alone,
Move slowly up to her,
Tap her on the shoulder,
Give it to her,
Then move fast away.

Or take the Valentine,
Type a note to her on the back,
And when she is not looking,
Slip it into her book —
And don't look, no matter what.
If she asks if you
Gave it to her,
Quietly say, "Yes, I did."

Tony Jacobson :: Grade 9
Swanville School :: Swanville

Once there was a really weird scientist. He was always fooling around with junk so he might make something that worked.

One day he was trying to make an invisible potion. When he finally got it to work, he tried it on his dog, Dufas. When it hit Dufas, the dog's paw started to get all wavy and the next second the dog was gone.

There was a neighbor boy that always was snooping around Franklin's house. He saw Dufas disappear, so whenever he saw anybody he told them about it.

The next morning the National Science Foundation President pulled up to Franklin's house in a long black limousine. When Franklin saw the car, he put on his white coat so he'd look more professional. When Franklin saw the president guy he was thinking, "What a nerd." Then the president guy said, "So you finally made something right. And don't just stand there, show me how it works."

So Franklin brought out his pet mouse Dudley and it worked the same as it did on Dufas. The president guy's head almost fell off, he was so impressed. But there was only one flaw. It only worked for about 8 hours. When Franklin sat in his easy chair, he felt something licking his face. It was Dufas.

The president guy called Franklin and said, "There will be a limousine in front of your house at 8:00 in the morning sharp. the chauffeur will drive you to the airport and you'll fly in my jet to Washington, D.C."

When the limousine came to Franklin's house, he was ready, and he even brought his briefcase. In about half an hour he was at the airport. He jumped in the jet as fast as he could.

The jet could go about 500 mph, so he got there in no time. When he got to Washington, he checked his briefcase so he had everything ready. When he got to the Science place, Franklin thought it looked like a huge castle. When the president guy opened the door, he said, "Now let's get started."

So they went to a big lab and tested all night. When the potion was gone, the president guy said, "So why don't ya make some more?"

Franklin said, "I forgot how."

And then Franklin got kicked out and was sent on a 24th class trip back home. But he never stopped fooling around with stuff.

Brian Rayhorn :: Grade 6
Long Prairie Schools :: Long Prairie

MELODY

Practiced hands
feel the cold smoothness
of ivory.
A single note
shatters the stillness.
Slowly building –
angry, exploding,
loud –
soft –
a light melody
sad and quiet,
slowing into
a final chord.
Practiced hands
close the cover.

Jodi Hauschildt :: Grade 12
Prescott High School :: Prescott, Wisconsin

The piano
is a huge
trunk with
wires shaking
inside.
Clean, shiny
white paint
with black
bruises.
Musical
symbols
confusion.
An ice cream
bar on a stick
where the chocolate
is gathering
at one end.
The keys chatter back
and forth, answering
each other, old friends.
After I've mastered
a hard piece
my fingers shout
Alleluias
You're my piano.
No one is allowed
to play but me
or animal sounds
occur.

Ann Walsh :: Grade 8
Kerkhoven-Murdock Secondary School :: Murdock

The silence of diving.
Slipping through
the water like a
worm sliding
through mud.
Skittering along
the bottom of the
ocean floor like a
hamster.
A big whale flies by like a silent jet.
Giant coral reefs like big
skyscrapers in the sea.
Bubbles coming from a rubber tube
like smoke coming from a factory.
Giant fish floating by like a
submarine.
Giant flippers propelling you further
and further into the ocean.

Stuart Francis :: Grade 6
Widsten Elementary School :: Wayzata

It's 6:00 a.m. I'm wondering why I'm in this locker room. The air feels like the inside of a sweaty gym sock, not to mention the smell. I'm starting to wake up as I tie my NIKE Airstabs so tight I can actually feel the laces cut off the circulation at my ankles.

I'm almost completely awake and preparing for the jolt of fresh air. BOOM it smacks me as I walk onto the cool indoor track. I start my stretching and watch some guys do some outrageous slam dunks. They look as if in mid-air they pop parachutes and move around in slow motion, then BAM! put the ball through the basket.

That's where I want to be, but I have five miles to run and some weights to lift. I get up and jog. I start to pass some slim, muscular, figures and I say I look like them, and I do. Except I'm 5'11" and have been since 7th grade.

I sometimes feel jealous and would give up my whole partnership just to be 6'6", but I realize how stupid that would be. I feel my rhythm skip once and realize I have one lap left.

I step into a weight room, loosen up and look at the human torture machine toward the center. Then I look again and realize I am surrounded by a group of 6'3", 250 lbs. guys screaming as they conquer the weights.

I walk towards the bench bar and I'm swooped off my feet. "Hey Big Guy, my little buddy, ready to pump?"

That's my best friend, Thor. Yes, his name describes him. 6'4", 276 lbs. all muscle, and my best friend. I hate it when he calls me that but it's a natural reaction for most people.

After an hour of body-breaking lifts I go out and stretch. I watch some guys play B-ball and a knot in my stomach tightens and breaks.

I go down to the court. "Hey, Livingston, get in here we need a point guard," Mike yells.

I get in there and regret my position. No matter how good a point guard I am, I'd like to play forward and be on the other end of one of my alley-oops.

I get to the other end of the court on defense waiting for my taller opponent to bring the ball. He fakes at me, then drives the other way, routinely I steal the ball for an easy break away lay-up.

All of a sudden I hear a whistle. "Boy you can get up there, why not dunk?" Mike says. I think he's kidding but I realize how high I was up there. They give me the ball and BAM! I slam it through. I can't believe it, so I try again, and BOOM! It goes through again. For once I have the feeling I'm as tall as everyone else, all I have to do is jump.

Suddenly I realize how relative tall really is . . . . Wait till I take it to the hoop next time.

Peter Griffith :: Grade 8
Caledonia Junior High School :: Caledonia

It was a nice summer day in the year 1975. My friend Mike and I were watching the dominant New York Knicks on television, just before we went out to play. Mike's dream was to be a point guard in the NBA. People doubted that he'd make it out of the ghetto, but the more they doubted the more determined he was. Every night we'd play basketball. We lived next to each other in an apartment building in the Bronx, New York. While we played basketball, our neighbors were using drugs, stealing and shooting. We were shooting, too, but we were shooting baskets.

I'll admit I wasn't much competition for Mike; in fact, every basket I made was a moral victory. I learned a lot by playing against him and since I was taller than Mike, he learned how to get position for rebounding and how to shoot over me. I would pretend I was Willis Reed of the Knicks and he would pretend he was Walt Frazier.

Three years later we started junior high basketball. Mike was the star of the team, he had 186 points in just 13 games. After every game, whether we won or lost, our team would fight the other team. Some of the players were more excited about winning the fight than if we won the game.

In eighth grade, Mike started for the varsity team, but would never brag about how good he was doing. He always said he couldn't wait until we would be able to play together again. While Mike wasn't the star that year, he did lead the team in steals and assists. This was a great feat for an eighth grader.

Mike and I got to play together when we were juniors. Before the games, a few people would take drugs. One day I saw Mike taking them and tried to stop him. He said, "I only take them once in awhile because it hypes me up for the game." Mike went over the 1,000 point mark in our first game that year. He also led us to the state championship with a few buzzer beating shots. We got second in the state tournament and finished with a 25-2 record.

In our senior year, Mike was getting scholarships from

many major schools and had publicity all throughout the East coast. He led our team to first place in the state championship and finished his high school career with 2,587 points. The year was 1984 and Mike had signed with Georgetown University. I was also there, but not for my athletic ability. Mike didn't play much his first year, but that was expected, since he was only a freshman. Georgetown won the NCAA championship that year.

Mike now hung with a whole different group of kids. I didn't see much of him that first year. He started a few games his sophomore year, but went out with a broken foot in his eighth game. He didn't play the rest of the year; we seemed to be growing further and further apart.

In his last two years at Georgetown, Mike led the team in scoring, steals and assists. He was the sixth pick in the first round for the NBA draft. It was the happiest moment of my life; I was so excited Mike's dreams came true. Mike came home that day to his family. His mom told him how proud she was that he had escaped the drugs and the gangs and had reached his goal.

Three days later, I picked up the newspaper and read that Mike had died of a drug overdose. He hadn't escaped after all.

Brody Schaefer
GFW West Middle School :: Fairfax

THE FROZEN POND

Across the frozen pond
in late winter,
in the woods
we had been building a tree fort and
spring was in the air.
Dusk was coming.
We plummeted down the pole
and started towards home.
Walking on the ice
we came to a crater.
The icy water down in the center of it
mirrored our reflections.
He was leaning over it
slipped and slided into it.
We laughed at his clumsiness.
Then, horrified, we watched him
slide back into the deadly water
after several times of trying to climb the slick embankment.
Panic crossed our faces.
We couldn't reach him.
He was desperate and pale now.
An idea came to me.
My heart pounding, I raced back to the Fort
ripped the pole out of the ground,
and charged back.
He was shivering.
He grabbed the pole which
was his lifeline.
We pulled him to safety
and rushed him home.
It was a cold walk home that night,
but I had a light burning in my heart.

Eric Hernandez :: Grade 10
Anoka Senior High School :: Anoka

Do You See Me

Do you see me mother,
    down here trying to make my way
        in life?
With laughter and girls

Do you catch how we live
    for the fun of it?
High heels and black socks
    going to a party
We'll drink a couple glasses
    before the night is through

Do you watch your girl-child's passion
    (the tussle and gleam of it)
As I learn to walk the lines?

Denise Anderson
Jefferson Alternatives :: St. Paul

CHRIS

You affect me like a hurricane
   does the land.
Your harsh words bring downpours
   to my heart.
When you ignore me, it is like
      tremendous winds throwing
      my dreams out to sea.
But then there are sunny days
   and I feel like I'm in heaven.
When will this hurricane end?
When will I have the strength
   to move to a safer place?

Eileen Christensen :: Grade 12
Battle Lake High School :: Battle Lake

THE POND

I remember sitting
with my best friend in the world
we are sitting at the edge of a pond at night
catching grasshoppers, frogs, and fireflies
the moon shines bright on the pond
the trees blowing leaves of all different colors
flying everywhere
throwing stones in the pond and telling secrets
and when it is time to go home
the pond is very quiet.

John Rosso :: Grade 5
Glen Lake Elementary School :: Minnetonka

I am the poet
who swims to the
treasure of light
and beings to
write. I am the poet
who falls in a rose
and thinks of a poem.
I am the poet who
boats to the writing
sun.

When I write my poems
the roses glow. When I write
my poems a child
cries under the stars.

When I finish my art
I give it to the
earth and nature
with love.

Mary Tse :: Grade 2
Normandale Hills Elementary School :: Bloomington

POOR ME

Poor me.
I'm so ugly
that when I look at the TV
it explodes,
When I look at a house
it breaks down,
When I look at a parade
it runs away
and goes to another place.
Poor poor me.

Danika Franklin :: Grade 2
Centennial Primary School :: Richfield

In Dreams

It's bedtime and I dream
I'm falling into a
strange hole like
Alice . . .

flying like a bird
with Mary Poppins . . .

being a hero better
than Robin Hood . . .

It's like being stronger
than Superman . . .

growing bigger
than Hercules . . .

having the wisdom
to be as smart as an
owl . . .

Just then, I wake
up an ordinary kid
in my pajamas.

Justin Gall :: Grade 4
Washington Elementary School :: Moorhead

Big rocks collide and shake me toward life.
Giants walking move me farther.
Great tidal waves crash to the ocean floor,
which raises me farther.
All of a sudden I hear a crack!
It is an earthquake, I can see Life!
A rainbow shoots down toward me,
it wraps around me and pulls me up.
I am Alive! I look at myself:
The rainbow has colored me red.
I look around: One by one,
the giants disappear,
Trees grow, plants grow, berries grow,
Rainbows dance around.
I am the son of wind and water.
I am swift and cunning.
I am Alive! I am the Fox of Red.

Corryn Trask :: Grade 4
Deer Lake Elementary School :: Bemidji

SELF PORTRAIT

I'm made of scraps and leftovers,
Things other people didn't want.
Whirling! Whirling!
I'm a design of nothing
With a dark confused blue,
A mean flashing red,
A deep hurting orange.
Things fly into my brain and go whizzing out again.
Nothing stays put.
People look at me and laugh.
The sky around me is a dark haunting black,
Getting darker every time someone teases me.
I try to lock out the feelings
But it seems they have a master key
to my ragged heart.

Heidi Zierdt :: Grade 5
Southview Elementary School :: Apple Valley

LIKE I SHOULD BE

When I am proud,
I turn into a butterfly
floating in the air,
singing a song,
being pretty like
a butterfly should be,
and if someone tries
to catch me
I will simply fly
away and away,
being pretty like
a butterfly should be.

*Erin Ulery :: Grade 2
Southview Elementary School :: Apple Valley*

UNTITLED

I am a child
of battle.
My soul is a
pile of anger.
My soul is a
broken down building.
My eyes are a lost
planet in space.
My life is a
deserted farm house.
My life is a jar full
of sad dreams.
The world is just
another drop of water.
My thoughts are forgotten
ghosts in the graveyard.

John Holder :: Grade 5
Eisenhower Elementary School :: Hopkins

preheat cranium to 400 degrees
divide thawed brain into 2 parts
color one part creativity
color one part originality
roll out both hemispheres on a flour-covered
surface until about one-fourth inch thick
cut into desired shapes
place along the walls of your mind
until golden brown

makes about 30 million thoughts.

Cortni Just :: Grade 8
Rush City Schools :: Rush City

Bugs

When I have too many
  projects to do and
    I don't have
      the time
        to do
          them

it feels like there is
  a spider crawling up
    into my
      brain.

It sounds like the Fourth
of July, or people laughing
  so hard they
    start to
      cough

or a dolphin trying
out for choir and a
    violin squeaking.

It is like my brain is
blowing up because it
    has too much
    information.

Sara Johnson :: Grade 4
Delano Elementary School :: Delano

The bassoon was playing softly
and the flute was weeping
most beautifully
The harp was trying to sing itself
to sleep.
The xylophone got hurt and was trying
to repair himself.
They woke me up
and I saw those instruments
doing what they were doing.
I told them to be quiet
and they did!

Rachel Steinberg :: Grade 2
Hale Elementary School :: Minneapolis

Farewell I'm leaving now
Farewell
trees
flowers
air
Good-by
every thing will change now
my brain
my lungs
My heart
Good-by
Good-by
Good-by
    rain
    lakes
    rivers
lollipops and shivers
    shadows
pools
    FAREWELL

Brent Dahlheimer :: Grade 5
Dayton Elementary School :: Dayton

MY NAME

My Name is like a shooting
star falling from the sky. It's
like a person running around the
whole world without ever slowing
down.

My name is like a wild horse that
has never been caught. My name
is like a sunny day that has no
clouds.

My name is like a swimmer swimming
the English Channel. My name is
like a track star that just won a
gold medal.

My name is like a baseball player
who has gotten the most home runs
in a career.

My name is like a meteor that went
through the atmosphere.

My name is like a bird that flies high
above the sky. My name is like a deer
that can run very fast.

My name is like a painting by a
famous painter that everyone admires.

My name is like the wind that can
blow very hard. My name is like a
fancy hotel that everyone comes to.

Jason Grove :: Grade 4
Armstrong Elementary School :: Cottage Grove

The hand so fragile
Like a hollowed-out egg shell
Nails made of glimmering crystals.
Knuckles that show peace
As they sit there patiently,
Wrinkles so tiny,
Showing not a care in the world,
So smooth,
As a freshly-sanded board
This hand is like the poor,
Not greedy or spoiled
This hand is the right hand,
The left hand is so strong,
Grasping the right
Like pliers to an object
The veins popping out
Hands so rough,
Like a tree after being struck by lightening
Hate and selfishness
Fighting its way through the blood stream.
These hands are kindness and anger
Kindness right
Anger left.

Chad Boldthen
LeSeuer Junior and Senior High School :: LeSeuer

TREES

I am the tree
in the hot
desert.
You are the little
man in the cold
ground.

I give you oxygen as warm as a light bulb
to breath.
You give me water as cold as clay
to drink.

Together we're a team.
We'll stay alive together.

Sometimes
you get cold
and cut
me down
for fire.
Then
you see
my ashes and
plant me once again.

Christopher Roberts :: Grade 5
Malone Elementary School :: Prescott, Wisconsin

A FRIEND

I am hard
You are soft
Drawn together
Though opposites
How it worked
You may guess
How it grew
You do know
How it broke
You should know
You are soft
I am hard

Julie Gambaiani :: Grade 7
Richfield Junior High School :: Richfield

Here is my friend Casie sitting by a tree. She is writing a poem that has quiet words in it. She is writing down about her family working with the leaves. While she is writing, she is listening to the birds sing. Casie loves the meadow she is in. She looks like she is a cat sitting by the tree. She's thinking of the quiet song the birds are singing. She is looking at the insect coming by. She thinks it's the beauty in her poem that makes the meadow as comfortable as home.

Kandi Peterson :: Grade 3
Malone Elementary School :: Prescott, Wisconsin

As she sits the aged floor cracks.

She opens the book and stares
with the calm of a lake perfectly still.

She picks up a pencil.
Her knuckles crack with the wear of decades.

She writes with the smoothness
of a bird in a slight breeze.

She sets the pencil down and gets up
from her chair as though she has quit.

She walks around the table twice
and sits once more.

She picks up the pencil and begins to write.

Kevin Pfeiffer :: Grade 10
Swanville High School :: Swanville

It probably was the thought of having so much power that drew me to this God-forsaken job. Now I wish I never had taken this calling. Sure, drivin' down the street and seein' people slow down has its perks. But by being a cop you get a lot of unwanted enemies. You know the type: a dumb punk who thinks he can rule the world just because he wears leather coats and blue jeans with slashes in the cheeks. But you get used to it. People givin' ya guff because you gave them a ticket for goin' 40 in a 35 zone is understandable, but the nicknames they give you: "Oh, no, it's the fuzz," or "That guy was a dick, I know it," or "Just because he's a pig don't mean he can tell me what to do! I can tell anybody whatever I want. I'm the law, and proud of it. It's like we're machines, not people. An accountant does his job, gets paid, and goes home. A straight 9–5 shift. A cop don't get the luxury of doin' that every night. Instead of havin' a beer, you have to stay by the phone and watch out the window so a nut case don't blow ya up. Why couldn't I have been a dentist? It's better pay, and you can always wash your hands after a job. The cop never washes away a case totally. You may have gotten the right man, but did you? Is it all worth it?

James Kleven :: Grade 8
Walnut Grove High School :: Walnut Grove

A Model to Look Up To

Walking slowly and deliberately toward a flower garden, Myrtle Chiglo encounterd a small, under-nourished puppy. She squatted down, bones creaking, and gently patted the dog's head. After a short time, Myrtle hurried back to the house. The starving dog followed her movement with sorrow-filled eyes, his heart breaking as she deserted him. Then the dog's tail began to wag rapidly as he saw Myrtle returning with a bowl of table scraps.

If a person looks into Myrtle's eyes, he can see the gentleness and compassion that she showed to the starving puppy. Even though she has led a hard life, Myrtle has also had happiness. The wrinkles on her face aren't frown lines but laugh lines, and Myrtle extends her kindness to everyone she meets.

Myrtle has resided in Whalan for fifty-nine years. Most of my life, I have lived across the street from Myrtle. She has always seemed the same to me — a sweet, old woman who has a heart of gold. Long ago, with her husband, Myrtle raised tobacco and managed a grocery store. They also owned a farm on which they milked a few cows and raised some hay. According to Myrtle, there weren't any tractors at that time. They used horses for the farm work and did the haying by hand. Myrtle said that there was never a surplus of crops on the farm. Whatever they didn't eat themselves, they fed to the horses. In Myrtle's own words, "Farming back then was the way the Amish farm now. It was a lot of hard work."

Because she grew up in this area, Myrtle feels as if she belongs here. Most of her family remains in this area, and this is where she spent her life with her husband. According to Myrtle, she really began to feel as if she belonged here when she was a young girl. At this time her father went blind, and the family was forced to leave the farm. They moved to Whalan where they lived for about four years. After that, the family returned to an area farm. Lacking eyesight, Myrtle's father was unable to do any of the farmwork, so he told the children how to do it. Myrtle, along with her brother and sister, did all of the farmwork. Often, the neighbors would help. The neighbors kept an eye on Myrtle and her family, making sure they had everything they needed. The family was always welcome at neighboring farms, and this is what made Myrtle feel a sense of belonging.

Looking back over the years, Myrtle remembers when Whalan was actually more prosperous than Lanesboro. At one time, Whalan had three grain elevators, a cheese factory, a stockyard, a lumberyard, a bank, a hotel, a post office, two garages, two grocery stores, and a restaurant. She also remembers the railroad. Many years ago, freight and passenger trains came through Whalan regularly. Myrtle sighed regretfully as she said, "It's a shame that there's nothing left here now." In Myrtle's opinion, the main reason for Whalan's loss of business was the closing of the school. Myrtle stated, "When the school was moved to Lanesboro, the business went too."

Myrtle feels that the old Whalan school and most other old schools had very good education, even though materials were sometimes lacking. She believes that she learned more in a country school than many kids learn today. Myrtle also said that students are much different today. When she was young, students enjoyed school more and looked forward to it. They obeyed the teacher and always tried to complete the assignments. Now, Myrtle believes, many students take education for granted and don't make good use of it. Today's students question the authority of a teacher and often disobey. According to Myrtle, students didn't dare disobey the teacher when she attended school because there was always the threat of punishment.

Myrtle believes that the future for Lanesboro, and even Whalan, is bright as long as the school remains in Lanesboro. Myrtle said, "I don't want to see the same thing happen to Lanesboro that happened to Whalan. They better keep that school." Myrtle also thinks that the state trail and the tourism industry will help Lanesboro survive and prosper, but she believes that everyone must work together and take advantage of these things. Myrtle stated, "We can't allow them to slip away or our community will die out. To make sure our future is solid, we must develop businesses which provide for the tourists' desires."

For the most part, I agree with Myrtle. I think this area can survive if the school remains, and we use the tourism industry to our advantage. If businesses which deal with the tourists' needs are set up, more money can be introduced into the economy. This would benefit everyone and help the town to survive.

Myrtle also believes that it's inevitable that the young people of our area leave. She said, "I only hope that they remember us and carry us with them in their hearts everywhere they go." I agree with Myrtle. It feels natural to me to be one of the students who will be leaving. In this area, there aren't many career opportunities for young people. I probably won't be able to work at a job of my preference in this area. I would like to continue to call this area "home," but I probably won't be living here in the future.

To me, Myrtle Chiglo symbolizes the type of person I would like to be. She's caring and kind. Those two traits are very important to me. Also, Myrtle is satisfied with her life. She doesn't dwell on the past but lives each day as it comes. From Myrtle, I have learned that hard work doesn't hurt anybody. It helps a person to grow and learn. In my eyes, Myrtle Chiglo is a model for all young people to look up to.

Andrea Rahn :: Grade 11
Lanesboro Senior High School :: Lanesboro

First, slap on a plastic smile
Then, add overwhelming eyebrows and flaring nostrils
Next, a firm handshake
And a fatherly attraction to babies
Next, mold together
Arrogance and a humor only he understands
Avoidance of reporters
And a great sense of when to change the subject
Cook to desired shape
For best results
Add big white teeth
And a strong arm for throwing mud

Ryan Rector and Steph Walters :: Grade 8
Hopkins North High School :: Hopkins

The shore,
a new place where we are going,
said Gram.
Is it a park, a movie, a game?
I asked.
> No
> It's a place where all things have come
> and gone, for ages and in dreams.
> A place of rest and refuge
> in the soft ocean breeze!
The tide of time flows across the soul,
and brings in the dreams from time.
> The shore.

Glenn Fletcher :: Grade 11
Prior Lake High School :: Prior Lake

. . . I opened the box. In it was a caterpillar. It twirled its head and we appeared in a world of gold. It told me to touch everything. I did. Everything I touched was alive. When I touched a lion, first it moved its eyes, then it moved its nose, then its tail, then it licked my face and ran away. It stopped and looked at me as if it wanted me to follow it. I followed its lead to 6 baby lions. They were gold too. I touched them. They came to life — they all licked me and I got to take one back with me.

Cyndie Brown :: Grade 4
Sand Creek Elementary School :: Coon Rapids

Once this weird playwright came and made us do all kinds of strange exercises. Suddenly all of the energy went to my feet and it burned a hole straight through the floor. Next I started floating straight down! I couldn't stop! And I looked up. I saw the school going farther and farther away! Finally I stopped. I looked around and it looked like I was in a Mystical Forest. It was all different colors. There was a misty fog on the ground and it felt like I was walking on clouds. At first, I was scared. Then I thought that I was dreaming! I heard a noise that sounded like whispering. Looking around, I saw a Pegasus. The Pegasus was beautiful! It was white with a silver mane and tail. Its white coat was gleaming and shining in the light. Its hoves were also sparkling silver.

"Who are you?" I asked, my fear leaving me.

"I am Misty" she answered.

"Where am I?" I asked. Now I was calm.

"We are in the Mystical Woods," she said. "Would you like to have a view of the forest?" she asked. I said yes and climbed on her back. She flew up and over the forest. It was even more beautiful from the top. At first I was a little uneasy flying, but then I got used to it.

I looked down and saw a clearing in the forest. I asked Misty what it was and she said it was the Mystical box of the Mystical Woods and no one in the forest had been able to open it yet. Only a human child could open it. She flew down and landed gracefully next to the box. The box was a big beautiful metal box with jewels sparkling on its sides.

"Would you like to try to open it?" she asked me.

"Sure, I'd love to!" I answered. Misty showed me where the key was. I picked it up, inserted it into the keyhole, and turned it. Magically, the box opened! A rainbow of colors shot out of the box, circled around, then shot back into the box. I looked into the box. It was empty! I told Misty it was empty and she said it can only do or be what you tell it to. I told it to go back to the classroom. Then I snapped my fingers and it disappeared!

I looked at my watch, school and was almost over. I asked Misty if I would ever see her or the Mystical forest again.

She said "Whenever you want to get here, go into your box, close your eyes, look deeply into your imagination and you will be here." The next thing I knew I was back in class.

Annie Vogel :: Grade 4
St. Wenceslaus Elementary School :: New Prague

I am climbing a mountain when a deer runs past just giving me a rope to climb with to the mountain top. It gets hard but the deer comes back to help. Soon I make it up the steep mountain. Then the deer trots down the mountain and soon goes out of sight. Soon after I get to the top, snow starts to fall down and brings me with it. So then I get up, but still sore all over. I have to climb again because I forgot to put the flag on top, so I start all over. Soon I reach the top and put the flag in the dirt but then I notice that I have the wrong flag so I carefully walk down and exchange flags and go back up. I finally do everything right.

Shawna Brenke :: Grade 4
Belle Plaine Elementary School :: Belle Plaine

My Secret Friend

I was in the park on the swings. It was a town picnic. There were over 3,000 people. Suddenly, they all disappeared. I was very frightened, until a ladder appeared. There were at least 55 steps. I went down—it was like paradise! There was gold, an ocean, and a girl. We swam for awhile. She told me to go back up. I was surprised. but, I still did go up. It happened again, this time she brought some toys, golden toys, and two gold horses.

Songkhla Tran:: Grade
Harriet Bishop Elementary School :: Rochester

My sister and I went over to my Grandma's house and slept over there. In the middle of the night we went outside. My grandma has a place with There was a whole bunch of woods. One night we had a dream that we went outside in the middle of the night and went in there. I was five. My sister was six. We went in there and saw the trees shaking and eyes glowing. There were a whole bunch of cats with glowing eyes. They were all black. We ran out of the woods and into the house. We tried to wake my Grandma up, but she wouldn't get up. Then we saw more black cats. So we ran out out of the house. We both were hiding. But they found us. So we ran home as fast as we could. When we got home, my mom was watching T.V.

Deedee Ferrence :: Grade 3
Centennial Elementary School :: Circle Pines

Once upon a time I was walking in a maze. I stumbled over a rock and when I hit the rock it opened a wall leading me into a sea monster cave. I thought it would be great if I went in and saw it. Before I did, I found an apple on the ground and I ate it. I was so hungry. I felt really sick and finally realized that it was poisoned. I got all the way in the cave and a flying chicken hit me and I fell to the ground and then the sea monster came and picked me up and threw me and I broke the wall and I found a whole bunch of diamonds.

The sea monster started to cry and he said, "How could you take my beloved treasure?"

"It's not yours is it?"

"No, but if you give me half the diamonds I will tell you about a young boy crying about not having any friends."

So the unicorn gave the sea monster half of the diamonds and he told the unicorn about the young boy named Do Do. While they were talking about the young boy, the young boy was crying about no one liking him.

Why won't anybody talk to me or play with me? Oh yeah, I am all by myself. I don't like it I really feel stupid. The only person I can talk to is myself. Boy, isn't that butterfly pretty. Man, look at the flowers, aren't they beautiful? Why won't anybody talk to me? Oh yeah, I keep forgetting, I am all by myself.

After me the unicorn found the little boy. I was talking to him. I said, "Well, look at the weather, wow. Ha."

"Yeah, really nice," said the young boy. He was really amazed that he was talking to someone else.

After I saw his enthusiasm, I said, "How would you like to become friends?"

"Sure that would be great." So finally after all the problems, the unicorn, sea monster and the little boy, lived happily ever after.

Jason Hartmann :: Grade 7
Princeton Middle School :: Princeton

When I fell down the tile, I bumped into a slimy slimy thing. It looked like a glob of goop, I got all sticky. So here I am as sticky as this thing and I look up and see another thing in the sky all furry. It bumped into me and now I'm sticky, slimy and furry. But that doesn't stop me so I keep on walking and come to a tree. The tree was talking to something. I looked around to see who it was talking to and I did not see anything.

"Are you talking to me?" I asked.

"Do you see anyone else?" he asked.

"No, but why are you talking to me?"

"Because I have something for you, climb up the tree."

So I climbed up the tree and saw a baby tree made of pure gold.

"Why are you giving this to me?" I asked.

"Because you are soooo boring and this tree will make you fun, wacky, and wild.

And when he said that all the trees and things started laughing, screaming, and going wild. Then I asked "What's going on?" And I was back in school. "Wow!" I said. I feel funnier already.

Sara Gunderson :: Grade 3
MacArthur/West Elementary School :: Duluth

THE MAN ON THE MOUNTAIN

Every morning I take a walk at six o'clock a.m. Well, one morning I was on my usual walk. The air smelt nice and fresh. This morning I decided to go for a walk in the Rocky Mountain. When I was walking I saw this man about ten feet in front of me, so I just kept on walking. When I was about three feet away I stopped. Now I could see that he had a long white beard, long white hair, and even a long white robe. I took two more steps forward. He looked at me in an odd way. I thought about this man for a moment. I couldn't stand the silence so I said, "What's your name sir?" He didn't speak, but I heard him mumble something. "What?" I asked in a small frightened voice. He said, "I'm the Angel of Bethlehem." "Oh, who is that?" I asked. "I'm the one who guards Jesus. Come with me. I'll show you." The guy held out his hand. I took it. In a few minutes we were standing over a cradle. The baby boy was crying. "We better go," said the angel. "You've got to go home." In a few minutes I was back at home in my bed. I thought for a minute. Was that really true? That question kept running through my head.

Christina Leisering :: Grade 3
Newport Elementary School :: Newport

Once a long time ago, a fox named Luke Foxtile lived. He always wore dark suits. He had white feet and the tip of his tail is white. His dark green eyes sparkle at everything.

His house was a hill. Inside he had three rooms, the living room, the kitchen, and his bedroom. In the kitchen there was a stove, a table, three chairs, a counter, a sink and cabinets. Weekdays, he went to the homemade furniture store.

One Saturday morning Luke was taking a walk through the forest. He thought he'd call on Zing, the famous turtle. Luke knocked on the door of his house. Zing, almost right away, answered the door. Apologetically he said, "So sorry I took so long. I was in the basement." "It's okay, may I come in?" "Why, of course. Come right in. I just made some pumpkin cookies. Have some with milk, won't you?" "Yes, yes! You know how much I love your pumpkin cookies." When they entered he continued, "I came here really because of a problem. You are so intelligent and all. You know that I live in that hill in the middle of the forest. I really don't like it. I'm quite tidy, you know, and I can't keep dirt walls, floors, ceilings or anything clean because, well, it's just naturally dirty. Would you have any ideas?" Zing thought for a moment. Then eventually said, "I have a wonderful idea! Why don't you build a new house? I could help you and I know most of the others would help, too." "Oh, what a brilliant idea. Let's get started right away. You go ask some of the others. I'll find things to build with."

They split up. Zing asked the rabbits, owls, foxes and turtles. They all helped. Luke found logs, bricks, stones, sticks and mud. Also he found the perfect place to build the house and with hard work with all the animals, they finished the house and moved everything into the house.

Amy Myers :: Grade 4
New Prague Elementary School :: New Prague

There was once an evil witch who came to a beautiful land and turned it gray. This land had a large castle, so she turned everyone inside into statues. After that she saw a young girl about 7 and changed her back so the girl could work for her. The girl's name was Mary and she didn't like the witch and wouldn't have stayed with her except the old lady had a dragon with her called Fred. Fred's name wasn't very bad, but he was. He would eat ten cows a day and chase Mary back to the castle if she went further than two miles away. The town was only a 1/2 mile away and Mary had a few friends there, although she didn't get to see them very often. If they came to the castle the witch was very mean to them and often Mary would get mad at her.

Once there was a party in the town she was planning on going to. That morning she had washed the steps but it had taken her an hour and the evil witch said that was too long. She then decided that Mary couldn't go to the party and Mary started to plan to do away with the witch.

That day Mary couldn't say anything for the witch had her magic wand with her and Mary knew what would happen if she made the witch angry. Once before she had made the witch mad and was turned into a frog for a day. So it seems best to keep on her good side if she has one. The one good thing Mary found from that was she knew the frog spell.

A letter came for the evil witch one day and it had bad news (for Mary that is). It said the witches were having their ten year reunion and Mary soon found herself on a train with the witch to the meeting. Mary had heard of these meetings and was frightened, so she formed a plan. That night on the train when the witch fell asleep Mary, who was wide awake (from drinking lots of coffee) tiptoed up to the witch and grabbed her wand. Quickly she mumbled the words "Smog Frog" and there was a great blue light around her. Then a puff of red smoke and a loud scream. Out of the smoke hopped a big ugly green frog. Mary was never happier in her life, so at the next city she hopped off and strided home. At the gate to the castle she met Fred who wasn't too happy to see her but for the first time Mary wasn't afraid to see him. Again she mumbled the words "Smog Frog." And the light appeared again but instead of red smoke it was yellow and out of it hopped a green frog. All of the statues began to move and then all were turned back to normal. Her mother and father were very happy to see her and threw a party in her honor in which they burned the wand and lived happily ever after.

Julie Larson :: Grade 8
Prescott Middle School :: Prescott, Wisconsin

ME AND MALINDA

It was a warm summer day. The birds were singing merrily and the flowers were in bloom in California.

As I was waiting for my new roomate Malinda, I was feeding my cat, Fuzzyball, and wondering what Malinda was like. Then suddenly, the door slammed open, my cat freaked out and hid under the bed. "I'm here," the large shabby woman said, "my bags are out in the taxi," meaning for me to bring them in.

I went out and got them. There were about five bags of who knows what. I finished bringing in the bags. I saw that Malinda had seized my cat and was filling up the bath tub. And was trying to force Fuzzyball into the tub.

I screamed and said, "What are you doing?"

She said that cats are dirty and she didn't want to get sick. I said in a little bit calmer voice, "Cats don't like water."

She said, as my cat was hanging onto the sides of the tub. "Your cat doesn't seem to mind." Then as I left the bathroom, I hoped my cat would survive. I decided to go to the mall.

When I got back, I could hear the hair dryer going. Malinda must be drying the cat because I could hear a yowling coming from the bathroom.

Five minutes later Malinda and the cat came out. Malinda had scratch marks and the cat looked like she had stuck her paw in a light socket. Her hair was standing straight up in the air.

I grabbed my cat and said, "This has to stop. My cat will go mad!"

I was a little worried about my cat getting along with Malinda. Then I felt Fuzzyball brush against me. I decided to take a nap. When I woke up, I could smell something cooking. It smelled like cat!

I ran out and screamed at her and said, "What are you doing?"

Malinda said, "I am making dinner."

And then in a quiet voice I asked what was for dinner. Malinda said, "Cat."

I ran back into my room, screaming. I came out at dinner time. Malinda took a bite of cat and slowly turned into a cat. First she got ears, then a tail. Then suddenly fur began to grow. Malinda was a cat. That is how I got my second cat.

Jenni Scott :: Grade 4
Folwell Elementary School :: Rochester

Pig Out!

Here I am in the kitchen. When I'm mad or bored, I hop into the kitchen. I might have a piece of burnt toast, but I mostly like to figure out Bill James stats with a calculator on the counter. I also like to have a tasty cheese sandwich with moist apple butter. Sour cream tastes fine plain but I like it better on a re-heated baked potato. I think I'll have a bologna sandwich now, even though it tastes like mayonnaise. I like chocolate cake better. I wish it was my birthday every other day so we can never have leftovers of chocolate cake. I wish that coffee maker will stop gargling. I feel better now. I'm not bored because there's so much to do in the kitchen. Bill James stats help me forget my worries. So you know I like to PIG OUT!

Mike Zimmerman :: Grade 5
Crestview Elementary School :: Cottage Grove

It was a nice cool day so I decided to take a walk along the beach. All I could think of was what a bad week I've had. Everything had seemed to go wrong.

Suddenly I looked up and in front of me stood a door. The door was not real tall. It looked like a door from a rich elegant house. It was dark brown with a brass knob. In the upper middle of the door was a brass knocker. On each side of the door were long narrow windows. In front of the door, was a cement step with a mat on it. Sticking half way out of the mat was a key. As I pulled the key out, I noticed it was an old tarnished key. It was not like modern keys, but rather, it was a long thin key with a small circle on the end to hang on to.

I decided to see what was beyond the door so I put the key in the key hole but it would not turn. As I was about to try to open the door again, I suddenly remembered when I opened another door similar to this one. It was my mother-in-law's door. And as I opened it, I saw a lot of ladies sitting in chairs crying openly and hugging each other because of the loss of someone very dear to them. Someone who was also very dear to me, my husband. The pain struck me so hard, I stood in front of the door with tears running down my face. Finally, I pulled myself together and tried once more to open the door. As I turned the key, the door slowly creaked open. I stepped inside the door wondering what I would see. When I looked up, it was as if spring had just arrived. There were birds chirping in the trees, green grass was growing everywhere and the sun felt warm on my face with only a little breeze. It seemed odd, because it was as if I was standing in my home town. I saw houses all around and children I once knew when I was younger were playing in the streets. I continued to walk around and everything I saw was a complete replica of my home town. Everything was the same as it was when I was in high school. Even the old grocery store with the Pepsi machine in front of it was still standing. The only thing different was me. I wasn't sixteen like back then, I was still thirty-five, the same age I was when I was standing on the other side of the door.

All I could think of as I looked around is that I must be dreaming. But I knew deep down I wasn't. Everything was so real. The people were real, the houses were real, and even the look of the bright blue sky with a few fluffy clouds was real. Nothing was strange or odd looking like it could be in a dream.

One thing kept bothering me though since I had realized this was Kinston, my home town. I wondered, if my house was still here. So I walked to Maple Street where I had once lived. Curious, yet afraid of what I would find, I slowly walked down the street. And as I looked up, I could see my brother Matthew playing basketball in front of the house. He was short and real skinny, but boy was he quick. Whoever would of thought he'd grow up to be so tall and muscular.

I must of been standing in front of the house for a long time because all of a sudden I heard someone asking, "Lady, lady are you O.K.?"

Seeing Matthew stand right in front of me startled me. I stepped back and answered him softly, "Yes, I'm fine. I was just walking around. I didn't mean to bother you."

"That's all right, you just looked lost. I thought maybe I could help you."

How could he not recognize me? I'm his only sister. The one he always turned to when he needed someone. I was the one who was there by his side when he woke up from his operation when he had his appendix taken out. I remember how scared he was.

"Lady, are you sure you're O.K.? I can go get my sister if you want. She's at her boyfriend's, it's only a couple blocks away. You stay here, I'll be right back."

"No, I'm fine. I'm sorry to bother you. I better go it's going to get dark pretty soon. Thanks anyway. You're a good kid."

As I turned away from him, I saw a bright light shining at the end of the street. I walked toward the light hoping to find an explanation for what I was going through. But once I got to the end of the street, I got more confused. To the right of me was Bruce Street. The street, Brett, my husband had lived on when he was a teenager. But to the left of me was an odd place. It was called KoKomo Street. I was positive there was no KoKomo Street in Kinston. Yet that's what it said on the street sign.

I started to journey down KoKomo Street. Everything seemed so sad. The grass was brown, houses were old and falling apart, and you could hear kids crying and adults fighting. There was even a lady digging in the trash. But as I got closer I noticed it wasn't just any lady, it was me. How could that be, I may have had hard times but nothing that bad. All of a sudden, I heard a gun go off and then I saw a cat run across the street. Three little kids were chasing it with a gun. Everything was too depressing and frightening for me, so I ran back to the end of the street.

Then, I decided to go down Bruce Street. It was like looking in a photo album. First I saw me and Brett going to our senior prom, then I saw the church we were married in. Next to the church was our first house, we were outside raking the lawn. Just then it seemed to get foggy. Although, I could still make out the people on the side of the street. I saw me and Brett washing our car. We sure had a lot of fun traveling in that car. Just as the street was about to come to an end, It started to rain. I saw a hearse parked on the side of the road. It was Brett's. He had gotten killed in a freak boating accident. I mourned for him for such a long time, I thought I was nothing without him.

All of a sudden, the hearse disappeared along with the fog and the houses. Sand was again squeezing through my toes. I turned around to see what happened and there, lying a few feet from me was Matthew's basketball.

I knew it wasn't a dream, it was real. It was a way for me to find out that I've had a good, successful life and I couldn't just throw it all away because of the loss of my husband. Compared to others, like those who live in the streets, I have everything. Brett may not be around anymore but I still have the rest of my family and friends. Maybe tonight when I get home, I'll call up Matthew and see if he wants to play a game of basketball sometime. Who knows, I might even beat him.

Tracy Houselog :: Grade 8
RTR High School :: Tyler

I hate peas. I've hated them ever since the others came. I used to love peas. Until I was marooned.

I was sailing on the SS Bummer to my cousin's house. My cousin's name is Diane, and she bears a striking resemblance to the Princes of Wales. She was on the SS Bummer with me.

SPLASH! Suddenly someone threw me overboard! They they PLENTY of bags and cans of peas after me, too. Everything went dank and dark.

The next thing I knew, I was washed up on the shore of a supposedly deserted desert island, and I was extremely exhausted, so I took a short, little nap. When I woke up it was nighttime, but I could just barely make out the lettering on the packages. I ate them raw for about a year.

Then one night I was awakened by the sound of harsh voices. After a couple of minutes I hid in the bushes. Then I could make out the figures. They look just like you and me, with spike-o hair, or they had mohawks. They wore chains and metal spikes on their leather jackets. They lifted their jackets over their heads and set them on the ground.

Then they each took a shovel out from behind themselves and started digging. And digging. And digging. They dug until the hole was five feet deep!

Then I saw the leader take a very noisy, big gigantic box out from behind her and put it in the hole. Then they filled the hole in.

They left, but the clumsier looking one dropped his shovel, so when they were out of sight, I ran and picked it up. I started shoveling. While I was shoveling, a million thoughts crossed my mind. At first, I thought the island was deserted, but now I wasn't so sure. I was wondering about what I would find in the box.

"I hope I don't have to eat *peas* for the rest of my life," I said loudly. I clamped a hand over my mouth. That was close, I thought. I dug some more.

I was very glad when I struck something hard. I dropped

the shovel and started using my hands. Then I pulled the big box out of the hole with my hands and opened it.

When I looked at what was inside, I thought, good-bye life. Nice knowing you.

I had just barely finished my sentence when everything went dark. Permanently. The box was full of frozen peas.

Jasmine Fredrickson :: Grade 4
Tilden Elementary School :: Hastings

"Hey, Dumbo," teased Max, the neighborhood leader, "Why don't you come over here and get your ears pierced?"

Lance pulled his baseball cap farther down over his head and slouched silently against the old oak tree at the corner of 5th and Banning.

"Flap those ears of yours and fly down here for a little fun."

Lance remained quiet, pulling his loops of hair over his ears. He turned his head away from Max to look in the direction of Marissa's house. "Where can she be?" said Lance with urgency.

"Come on, dumbo! I *know* you can hear me!"

Lance's heart began to beat rapidly. He wished Marissa would come right now. He didn't want to be alone here anymore. Lance began to fidget and bite at his lip nervously. He gasped for air and fought back unwanted tears. "What . . . what am I gonna do?"

"Psst!" said a hushed voice out of nowhere.

"What?" Lance looked about, confused.

"Psst! Hey, you down there," the voice whispered. "Do you need help?"

"Where? What? Who?" Lance caught sight of two owl-like eyes peering at him from between the leaves of the oak branches above him.

"Never mind the details. Do you want help or not?"

Lance nodded.

"Then hurry! Don't be so slow about coming up!"

"How?"

"What are you wait—Did you say something?"

"How am I supposed to get up there?"

"Oh," the voice said, sorry. There's some board steps nailed up the back of the tree."

Lance pivoted on his heels and quickly ducked behind the other side of the wide trunk. Scurrying up the ladder, Lance hoisted himself onto the sturdy wooden platform secured between three limbs.

"Thanks," Lance said to the back of the person kneeling down and peeking over the edge of the board. He could now see that the voice had come from a girl with strands of long hair that hung like a thick rope down her back. "Shh!" she hissed, motioning him to come over.

Lance scooted over, and lay at her side. "What's down there?"

"Max has no idea where you went. See? He thinks you disappeared into thin air."

(continued)

Michele Scheib :: Grade 11
White Bear Lake Area High School-South Campus :: White Bear Lake

The figure crouched low in the bushes as he looked over the park. His quarry sighted, two silhouettes against the moonlight, walking side by side. His eyes darkened as they followed the pair across the sand onto the swings. His teeth clenched as moonlight gleamed off the steel that was drawn from his pocket.

Jesse opened his blue eyes. Sunlight poured from his bedroom window. Sitting up from his bed, he rubbed his brown hair, vaguely remembering a scream in the midnight. "Sounded like a person," he said thinking aloud. "Probably just a cat." He dismissed the fright and stepped to the floor.

★   ★   ★

Jesse shouldered his book bag and hopped onto his ten-speed. He rode out of the driveway and down the street toward his school. Suddenly a police car with its sirens on roared down the street, past Jesse. Following it closely was an ambulance, its lights screaming. Jesse stared, stupefied, down the street after the two vehicles that continued down the road and turned a corner.

Jesse pulled over and checked his watch. He was ten minutes early. He was still mystified by the surprise, and wanted to check it out. The sirens had been silenced, proving that the police had stopped somewhere near.

Switching into a higher gear, he pedaled faster down the street and turned the corner. Coasting, he searched the sides of the street. He braked up by the children's park. There the police cars were lined up. A small crowd of bystanders were crowded near the curb. Jesse glimpsed one of his friends.

"K.C.!" he shouted. A fourteen-year-old boy turned around. "K.C.!" he called again. "What the hell happened?"

"Dunno." K.C. answered. "Someone's dead, cops wouldn't let us see 'em. But from the looks of the covered body, he looks about our height. Someone's going to get busted."

"No kidding." Jesse mumbled as he watched the medics raise the body up into the ambulance.

"Oh God!" complained K.C., "We're gonna be late!"

Jesse ran to his bike, followed in suit by K.C. Jesse tore down the street and rounded the corner. He almost forgot he had just bought a new bike. It was a twenty-speed and cost $500. Jesse felt serious about bike racing and he had always been riding fast. He was glad for the chance to test the limits of his new bike and himself, for he never had ridden it as fast as he could before.

He turned a corner and dodged a crossing cat. He glanced at his computer speedometer—only 30. He approached a hill and switched to a higher gear. Pedaling hard, he rushed down the hill. About to check his speedometer, he realized he was about to pass his school. Turning sharply, he pulled up his front wheel and jumped the curb. As he got a couple feet of air, he pulled up too far, landing on his back wheel. Slipping off his seat, he luckily landed on his feet, preventing a crash. As he walked his bike over to the bike rack, his friend Shea came over.

"Beautiful," he commented, then looked at his vehicle. "New bike?"

"Not for long," quipped Jesse as he locked his bike. Then K.C. appeared on his dirt bike.

"Nice moves," he laughed," you should try free styling."

"Yea, right. Let's go, we're late" Jesse answered.

"Late!" exclaimed Shea. "You're ten minutes early!"

Jesse glared at K.C. who grinned sheepishly. "Ooopppss, guess my watch is a little off." Jesse turned toward the door as K.C. adjusted his timepiece.

★ ★ ★

Jesse yawned. "Great," he thought, "tired in the first period." Eighth grade teachers were so boring this year. He glanced at the clock. Five minutes left. He peered around the room, but his gaze lingered on Michelle Steller. She had a strange look on her face. She just gazed out the window with wistful, kind of a sorrowful look in her eyes.

The bell rang with a piercing screech. Jesse watched Michelle slowly gather her books and sulk to the hallway door.

"Michelle!" called Jesse. She appeared not to hear. Jesse caught her in the hall, and waved a hand in front of her face. "Hi, Michelle."

As if she had never noticed him before, she acknowledged him nervously. "Oh . . . .Hi." she answered shakily.

"You OK? You look kinda spaced out."

Michelle forced a smile, "N-no . . . why? I feel fine."

"Man you look bad! Hey! I know, Greg's not here! Don't feel so bad, it's only a-"

"Look," interrupted Michelle angrily. "I gotta go." She hurried down the hall.

"I saw it all." Shea had come up behind Jesse. "You interrogated her. She ought to slap ya. What did you say?"

"Nothing!" said Jesse angrily as he elbowed Shea in the ribs.

★ ★ ★

After gym period, Jesse walked into the locker room, showered, and went to his locker to change. K.C. and a friend named Steve were laughing over a conversation that was interrupted to greet Jesse.

"Yo, Jess!" exclaimed Steve. "How's it going? I saw you outside today. You're real good, especially on curbs."

"You know it! What's going on?"

"Did you see the fight last Friday?" asked K.C.

"Fight?" asked Jesse.

"You mean you haven't heard?" demanded Steve.

"No! Don't keep me in suspense! Tell me!" exclaimed Jesse.

"Okay, okay. Just—Chill out," said Steve. "Here's what happened. As you know, Alan Burlop and Greg Talstad have hated each other for a long time. Many years in fact."

Yea, go on," pressed Jesse.

"Well one day, an argument broke out in the hall between them. Alan had Greg in a head lock and threw him against the wall. Greg staggered up and whaled Alan in the stomach, then pushed him down. Suddenly, Jeff, one of Alan's few friends, jumped up and shouted as loud as he could. "I'll kick your butt, Talstad!!" Greg just turned around and laid a solid blow, right on his jaw!" Steve hit his hand. "Jeff fell down right there. By then, Alan had come up behind Greg and got 'im in a choke hold."

K.C. continued, "Lucky for Greg, Steinberg arrived," he shook his head. "Of all the teachers that could have found out, it had to be him! Greg, Alan, and Jeff got a week's suspension."

"What was the argument about?" inquired Jesse.

"That's the weird thing," commented Steve "nobody, not even Steinberg could find out."

"Hmmm . . . ." mumbled Jesse, his chin on his hand.

The bell rang, Jesse was still half-dressed. With a shout, K.C. and Steve left for their next class.

Jesse hurried too, but in his haste, he tripped over his wet towel and fell to the wet floor with a groan. About to get up, he caught something out of the corner of his eye. He looked under his locker. The lighting was bad, so he couldn't see very well but he thought he could see the dim outlines of what appeared to be a knife.

★ ★ ★

At the end of the day, Jesse walked to the bike rack, where he met his girlfriend, Abbie.

"Hi, Jesse," she called.

"Hey, how are you?" he answered cheerfully.

Abbie giggled. "I saw you outside this morning. You're very talented."

Jesse rolled his eyes as Abbie laughed. "Who else knows about this?"

"A lot of people," she laughed, "Just think, you're a popular cyclist."

"Great," he said, "I feel better already."

"Listen," said Abbie, "I wanted to talk to you about Michelle."

"Yea," inserted Jesse, "I noticed she looked kinda screwed up. What happened?"

"I tried to talk to her," she answered. "She was close to tears. She kept saying to just forget about it, and not to get involved." She sighed. "After that she didn't talk to me at all."

"I guess I'll have to talk to her tomorrow. Going to the party Friday?"

"Of course," answered Abbie.

"Be ready to go by ten o'clock, okay?"

"All right, see you then. Good-bye," said Abbie.

"Bye," answered Jesse as he walked towards the bike rack. Just then, Alan walked up.

"Hi, Jesse," he called.

"Oh . . . . . . .hi," answered Jesse, then he asked." "Where's Jeff?"

"He needed surgery on his jaw because of last Friday," Jesse had a questioning look on his face. "You know, the fight?"

"Oh, yea. Listen, Alan, I gotta go. See you tomorrow.

G'bye. I hope Greg is —" suddenly Alan turned around and walked off.

"Yea, see you." Jesse called. He bent down to work his lock. Suddenly, after a few seconds Jesse thought. "Wait a minute . . . .Alan!" he shouted, turning around. But Alan was nowhere in sight. "But . . . ." Jesse thought out loud. "Naw," he laughed. "I gotta be dreaming."

★ ★ ★

The next day, during homeroom a single announcement came over the eighth-grade loud speakers.

"This is principal Steinberg, and I carry sorrowful news. Yesterday morning, a body was found in the children's park on Holland Avenue." Michelle suddenly stiffened up like a bolt, all eyes passing to her as the speaker continued. "Police identified the body as an eighth-grader, Greg Talstad." Sobbing, Michelle ran from the room, followed out the door by Abbie. Jesse, alarmed looked over at K.C. who formed the words "Oh shit" with his lips, Jesse quickly put a finger to his lips. A loud gasp came from the classroom. The speaker continued, "His body was stabbed twice, and cut across the neck. His funeral services will be held on Wednesday. We will call the school day off, so everybody who wishes may go. Please, if anyone has any information regarding this tragedy, please let us know. We will report it to the police." The speaker finished. The class was in an uproar. Elbowing his way through the crowd, Jesse drew K.C. by his arm and led him out of class.

In the hallway, K.C. was speechless. "G-G-Greg!" D-Dead!?"

"And Alan is absent today," Jesse stated.

"Jess, what is going on?!" exclaimed K.C.

"Listen, shut up about the body we saw yesterday morning." warned Jesse, "I think I'm on to something, and you could ruin it all by telling anyone."

"But who killed Greg?" asked K.C.

"I'm not sure, but I have an idea." Jesse turned around, and there he saw Michelle approaching. "Michelle . . . "

"Jesse," she said, "we need to talk."

"No kidding. Let's go." Jesse led Michelle to a storage room as K.C. went back to his homeroom.

Once inside, Jesse asked, "Where were you two nights ago?"

"Well," she said nervously "I was walking in the park with Greg. My parents didn't know, I just snuck out. I don't remember what time it was, but we sat down. I heard a crack behind me. Greg looked and it was a figure dressed in black. It was carrying a knife. Greg jumped up and hit it before it could could slash him. Greg shouted for me to run home and call the police. I got home and called them. We must have been out late, because by then it was morning. I just sat at home and waited. I couldn't go back, I didn't want to find out what happened. So I decided to let the police tell me." Michelle was in tears. "They never came. Oh God, I didn't know what to do!" Michelle fell into Jesse's arms, sobbing. He held her close, comforting her, then continued.

"What about Alan?" he inquired.

"Ohhhh . . . He was so hurt in school. Last year, I felt sorry for him, and I tried to comfort him, to be a friend. Next thing I knew, I was going out with him. He seemed so much happier then. I was glad that I had helped him out. Then . . . I started to notice Greg. He seemed so nice, so much more desirable compared to Alan. Then it happened—he asked me out. I was already going somewhere with Alan that night. I said 'yes' and told Alan I was doing something else with my family and canceled our date. When he found out the next day, he was so hurt. Alan didn't come to school the next day. When he came back, he wouldn't talk to me at all."

The bell rang again. Jesse snarled, he was tired of hearing bells. Releasing Michelle, he said. "Now, don't tell anyone about this little talk we had."

"Okay, 'bye" she answered, quivering.

"Good-bye Michelle. And hey . . . " he grabbed her arm, "don't worry, I'll get 'im."

"Thanks, Jesse, and be careful," Michelle turned and walked down the hall.

★   ★   ★

At the end of the day, Jesse went down to his gym locker. He put his backpack in his locker. Then he looked under it. He could see better now. It was definitely a knife, caked with dried blood.

Jesse got up, and walked to the door. He walked out and looked out the window. He felt a hand on his shoulder. He turned around, as a fist collided with his jaw.

Jesse hit the ground with thud. He could only see a blurry figure running down the hall and out the door. Jesse gasped, only the strength of his anger brought him to his feet. He stumbled out the door and to the bike rack. Grabbing his bike he pedaled down the street. He could see a figure speeding ahead, about a block away. Jesse pedaled hard. The figure turned right.

Jesse followed, only twenty feet away now. His antagonist headed for the park again, heading straight for the curb. Just after the curb, a low fence about two feet high surrounded the park. With his dirt bike, he easily jumped the fence.

Jesse speeded up, clenched his handle grips, pulled up, and prayed for no impact. He clutched at nothingness as he arced up over his handle bars and landed with groaning impact.

Jesse lifted himself and felt a warm liquid on his arm. His arm had been slashed by the fence. The figure ahead running into sand, had to abandon his bike. Jesse caught up with him easily and with one smooth motion, tackled him. Jesse gasped as he saw the astonished face of Alan. Jesse punched at Alan, who fended off the blow. Alan then landed a solid punch on to Jesse's nose. Jesse fell to the earth heavily. As he lay groaning, Alan grabbed the bike and took off.

Jesse picked himself up. He realized that he must retrieve the knife from school and turn it in to the cops.

Jesse stumbled back to his bike and inspected it. It had many scrapes and dents, plus a couple of broken spokes. It was otherwise rideable. Before he left, Jesse tore a long strip from his sweatpants and wrapped it around his injured arm. He mounted and rode off. By that time it was near dark.

Jess arrived at the school. A basketball team was practicing so the locker rooms were still open. Jesse entered the room. He kicked the lock off one of the lockers and opened it. Inside he saw many things, including a backpack. He took the backpack and dumped its contents onto the floor. He looked under his locker. The knife was still there. Jesse used the backpack to drag the knife away from underneath the locker. Gingerly grabbing it by the edges, he placed it into the bag. Jesse closed the bag and left the room.

Jesse left the parking lot and turned toward town. He saw no need to ride fast so he took it easy. He was glad for a moment of rest. Still clutching the bag, he leaned on the handle bars. Suddenly, a dark shape on the ground loomed in front of him. He swerved out of the way just in time. As he looked at it, the shape took on a human form. Jesse got off his bike and inspected the body. Moonlight played over the unconscious features of Michelle. Jesse almost fainted from the shock. Michelle was beaten over the head twice. Two large tell-tale bruises appeared on her temple. Jesse looked around. Nearby lay a large baseball bat. He realized that her house was just a block away. She was probably lured out and beaten. He also decided that Alan had found out about the talk in school. And that Alan was probably on his way to the school to retrieve his knife.

Jesse picked up Michelle and ran her to her house. He banged on the door. Michelle's mom and dad appeared at the door in their bathrobes. Mrs. Steller gasped when she saw her daughter.

"I don't have much time." The words tumbled from Jesse's mouth hurriedly. "Call the police and tell them to go to the school. The person that hurt Michelle is there. Call an ambulance. "Also," he added, "give this to the police," handing them the bag.

Mr. Steller looked shocked and confused, as Jesse continued. "Inside is the weapon the guy used to kill her boyfriend, Greg. Hurry, there's little time."

With that Jesse ran to his bike. He pedaled harder than he had in his life. Ignoring the danger, he jumped the curb on his right. He landed easily. Cutting through a yard, he switched gears. Jesse stumbled on the pedals. He did not realize his makeshift bandage was soaked with blood and dripping.

Jesse approached the school and leaped off his bike. The doors were closed but the glass was shattered and the lights on inside. Entering, he ran into and down the hallway. He then ran towards the locker room.

As Jesse ran in, he found himself staring in the muzzle of Alan's twelve-gauge shotgun.

"Where's the knife?" Alan demanded.

"Safe," Jesse answered calmly. "Out of reach for now."
Alan's face seemed to twitch with anger. Jesse continued.

"Why, Alan, WHY?! Killing Greg? And hurting Michelle like that. You loved her once. Now you're destroying yourself."

"MEEEE!!!!????" Alan screamed, "I'm destroying myself? No, Jesse you are wrong. So wrong." Alan turned livid, shaking so much he almost dropped his gun. "It was Greg, GREG! He ruined my life. He was my friend. A long time ago. Then he betrayed me. And my trust! He let everyone know all about me! All my secrets! Nothing was safe! He told my secrets!! Secrets that I had entrusted to him!" Alan tried desperately to calm himself.

Jesse felt weak. He realized he had lost too much blood. "Just kill time 'til the cops get here," he thought to himself.

Alan continued, "After that I looked like the fool, the outcast!! Sure, people were friendly half the time, but every time someone looked at me, I could feel them wondering about me, not trusting me! No one could trust me! I could trust no one! Then I found a person who understood, who cared! It was Michelle."

Jesse felt his vision blur. Alan still went on. "Greg even took her, I had nothing left."

"So you went out and killed him," forced out Jesse.

"Nnnnnoooooo!! He killed me! I knew he'd do that to others after me! I saved many."

You didn't help out your relationship with Michelle, by beating her. She'll never care for you again." Jesse felt deathly weak as his vision blurred further still.

"Nnnnnnnooooo!!! You don't understand!" Alan was in a frenzy now. but Jesse no longer cared as he crashed to the floor, unconscious.

Jesse woke up in a hospital bed. He saw a blury face above him. The split images connected to reveal K.C.

"'Bout time you woke up! Doctor was worried."

"Wha-Wha!" stammered Jesse.

Shea, Abbie, Steven and a doctor came in. K.C. turned around. "Here he is, guys."

Abbie clasped Jesse's hand. "You'll be OK. Thank goodness. You lost a lot of blood."

"Wait, where's . . . ."

"Well, in case you are wondering," said Steve, "Michelle's OK. She's gotta fractured skull, but Doc says she'll be OK."

"But . . . "

"Alan got nailed," cut in Shea, "Cops shot him just as you lost it."

"You mean everything is OK-", Jessie tried to sit up, but the pain in his head forced him down.

"You'll have to leave," said the doctor, "He needs rest."

"Let's go," said Steven.

Abbie clenched Jesse hard and whispered in his ear, "Welcome back. I'm so glad you're OK. The party was terrible without you."

Everyone left and Jesse sighed. Suddenly Shea poked his head in.

"Say, Jess, one question. How did you lose Alan at first? On your bike?"

John Matthew Aldag :: Grade 6
Blake Middle School :: Hopkins

THE ROBBERY

Staci was wondering what to do that night, since Johnny was working. Ring! Ring! "Johnny!" thought Staci as she picked up the phone. "Hello, Staci speaking," she said into the mouthpiece. "Staci? Can you fill in tonight? Rina's sick and Marie's in Chicago." It was her boss, Mr. Johnson. "Well, can you hang on a second? I'll have to ask," she said. Staci was a sub for Come-n-Go, a Stop-n-Go like store. "Mom! Any plans for me tonight?" Staci called down the bannister. "No, dear. It's your night" said Staci's mother, who was a trim 35 year old mother. She was, as Staci's friends would say, "the coolest mom ever invented." "Can I work for Mr. J tonight?" "Yes, dear." "Thanks!" Staci replied as she ran back to her room. "Mr. J.? I can. What time?" "In thirty minutes. Can you be here?" he asked. "Sure! See you then! Bye!" Staci hung up, dashed around looking for her clothes.

Fifteen minutes later she emerged from her bedroom wearing dark jeans, a crisp white shirt, white socks over her jeans, and red, slim dress shoes with her hair pulled back in a high ponytail. She was all set. She grabbed her keys and jean jacket. "Bye, Mom!" she called over her shoulder. She got into her car and drove to Come-n-Go.

"Hi, Mr. J.! How's business?" she asked. "A little slow. I would fill in tonight but I promised Mildred supper and a movie out. Women!" he muttered. Staci smiled. She knew Mr. J. thought taking out his wife, Mildred, was a pain. "Well, see you later, Staci," he said, grabbing his jacket and leaving. Staci sat down on the stool behind the counter and began adding up the sales.

After fifteen minutes, Staci looked up and began to look for customers who might have slipped in. She saw some apple tarts laying on the floor. She went over to pick them up. She hated a messy store. As soon as she bent down to pick them up, she felt a hand close around her mouth. A gruff voice said, "Don't scream or anything unless I tell you to. Got it?" Staci nodded her head. "Good." If I let go, do you promise not to run or yell?" Again, Staci nodded her head. The hand uncovered her mouth and Staci turned around, face to face with a medium tall man, sandy blonde hair and deep blue eyes. The man was holding something in his left hand. Staci looked down, a gun! Staci almost screamed. "You want money, right?" she asked. "Smart girl. Let's go get it," he said. Staci led the way to the counter. Oh no! thought Staci, as she saw Mrs. Arneson coming through the doors. "Quick!" said Staci. "Take off that ski cap." The robber took it off, went to the back of the store, and started walking through the aisles and picking up stuff, like he was shopping.

"Hi, Mrs. Arneson! How's Billy and Amiee?" asked Staci. "Oh fine. Billy is as big as ever, and Amiee just turned thirteen and she's being a typical teen," Mrs. Arneson said smiling. Staci chuckled to herself. "Oh, Staci? May I have a cup of coffee and a jelly doughnut, please?" "Sure, Mrs. Arneson," she replied. She rang up the items and gave Mrs. Arneson her change. "Just a moment, please," she said to the robber, who was waiting for Staci to ring him up. Staci turned her back to get Mrs. Arneson's doughnut. "So, Mrs. Arneson, how's your husband? I heard he just got promoted to sergeant." "Oh, yes. He's just as happy as ever." Staci saw the robber turn pale. She smiled. Staci had an idea. It might work.

Staci poured Mrs. Arneson's coffee. "Would you like some?" Staci asked the robber. "Yes, please," he said. Staci poured his coffee. As she turned around, she flung it towards the robber, and before he knew what was happening, Staci grabbed the coffee pot and threw its hot contents on the robber's face. He screamed, as Mrs. Arneson watched, astonished. Staci grabbed the gun they kept under the counter, pushed the burglar alarm, jumped over the counter, pushing the screaming robber down. Staci put her foot down on the robber, pointed the gun at his head, and yelled, "Don't move DirtBag! You even flinch, and I'll blow your brains out! Mrs. Arneson, grab some rope in the parts section!" "You wouldn't dare shoot me" he said. "Try me" Staci challenged. "OK," he said. He grabbed Staci's leg, pushed her foot off him, got up and ran. Staci clicked the gun, closed her eyes, and pulled the trigger. BAM! OUCH! Several groans followed. Staci opened her eyes and saw the robber laying on the floor, clutching his thigh, withering in pain.

Staci was thankful for the sound of sirens. Staci turned around and fainted. When she came to, people were all over. When she tried to sit up, a firm hand pushed her down. "My head" she muttered. In ten minutes, she found out she had shot a man named Robert Fordall, a small time robber, in the thigh. Staci was given a reward for saving Mrs. Arneson's life, and the store by catching a convict. Staci was made manager of Come-n-Go. Later that week, Johnny proposed to Staci and Marie Tomas, but that is another story. The End.

Summer Rosenfeldt :: Grade 7
Robert Asp Elementary School :: Moorhead

Life is hard now, but you be as mighty as
the house you live in.

You be as pure as the water
that runs through that mighty house.

Let you be as sturdy as the stairs you walk on.
When I pass on you will take care of this house
in my memory.

You will cherish this house like the genuine gold
locket you received on your 13th birthday. But all I ask
is that you keep my spirit in your memory.

Keep this house running strong like a recharged
battery as long as you can. I will be thankful for that.

Keep yourself going, don't fall on those stairs
and start to crawl. When things get hard, stay in
there and fight for what's yours.

I have never known you to give up. Don't even
start now. Hopefully this house will be passed
down from generation to generation, forever.

Chantelle Wise :: Grade 6
Webster Magnet School :: St. Paul

DOLPHIN

At first the oceans
were still and boring,
the fish were lazy,
the only things moving
were the plants in the sand
on the bottom of the sea.
Then a plant burst.
The thing from the plant
saw all of this
stillness and laziness.
He began to swim,
and the water began moving,
and the fish became wild.
That's when the thing
knew what his name was:
He was Dolphin.

Matt Bergwall :: Grade 3
Southview Elementary School :: Apple Valley

Baked mud, hot day, blackbird
lying in the garden.
    Let it live.

Found in brown grass,
fell out of the tree
    Please don't die.

Held it in my cupped hands,
gave a little push.
    Please do fly.

Finally got airborne,
never saw again.
    Live long.

Brett Anderson :: Grade 6
Norman County West Elementary School :: Hendrum

MY ANIMAL POEM

Oh, animal, you
make my hair
stand up like
scales. Then
when you roar
as the thunder of
the night,
my feet are stiff
as pigs.
When your antlers
turn in, my ears
go with them. You
are a moose
and you are
caught by the
moon at night.
When the man
on the moon
says, come to
me, as you
come, I change
back to my
self again.

Stacey Friedrich :: Grade 4
Holdingford Elementary School :: Holdingford

    The reflection of
the window
    The reflection of the
window on her glass
    the sound of the
piano
    the bearded man.
    To me a good pony
    is the most important
thing in the world.

Alicia Ciampi :: Grade 7
Lake Country School :: Minneapolis

THE SURVIVOR

The wolf is the Survivor.
    He is the one who takes
    the remains like free money
    being given to a robber.

At the fight he will conquer
    like the king on his throne
    and tell all his followers
    who the leader really is.

At the end of all he will
    howl at the moon, as if
    it was the only thing stronger,
    and waits for the day the moon comes
    down to fight.

Jason Sokolik :: Grade 7
Oltman Junior High School :: St. Paul Park

Cows

Cows
huge cows, beautiful cows
when they moo, thunder roars
don't get close
their feet are as big
as an elephant's foot
horns pointy like a pin.
Cows have large bones
an unbearable sight
cows
huge beautiful cows.

Tanya Hommerding :: Grade 4
Horace May Elementary School :: Bemidji

Boomer, you are so large,
you squash me to pancakes
when you sit on me.
You eat as much as the giant
in Jack and the Beanstalk.
You are so fast,
fast as lightning.
Your teeth are like knives.
You weigh as much as a ton of hogs.
Your tail wags so hard,
it knocks over trees.
You dig so deep,
you dig to China.
You are as tall as a stool.
O Boomer, O Boomer,
you're too big!

Shallyn Tipler :: Grade 4
Diamond Path Elementary School :: Rosemount

Riding in complete darkness.
I feel the darkness pressing in.
At the end of the lonely earth there
are tiny white sparkles growing in the darkness,
growing bigger by the second. They go
speeding past and another set of diamonds appear
as they get closer with each sparkle they
blind you with delight or anger. Then
suddenly there are no diamonds, no lights. Then just
as they left they appeared in the sky with
their master the biggest of them all.

They try to tell us something by putting
messages in the sky. At the end of
the horizon there is a different light.
It is the sunrise!

The diamonds start to disappear
and a much bigger diamond comes into
the world and a new day.

Travis Salisbury :: Grade 4
Lincoln Elementary School :: Bemidji

When I touch
        something smooth
                and super soft
                        I remember my
                                old dog Rusty
                                        who is now
                                                dead. Who
                                        got hit by a
                                car in late
                        January of '85
                late about eight.
        A drunk driver
tried to make him
        into a pancake or
                something flatter than a
        mud pie. We didn't even
                know until the next
                        day when we called
                                him out to play and
                                        Dad said he
                                                can't come out
                                                        or play today
                                                he won't even
                                        be hungry this
                                morning. Until then
                        I didn't know
                what had happened
        until I figured it out.

A little bit by
Then I felt
like crying, but
it was true
he was dead
flat or not!

Kristie Meyer :: Grade 4
Lincoln Elementary School :: Bemidji

SILENCE

At night
when the dreams
are like ballet dancers
in a child's head,
black cats
purr very softly.

Lea Graf :: Grade 2
Hale Elementary School :: Minneapolis

THE RABBIT

Night is still and cold.
The rabbit's ears bounce up like a ball,
His pink marble eyes look around.
Then rabbit runs as fast as lightning,
he runs through shrubs
while their fingers reach out and touch
his soft cotton fur.
Rabbit pauses,
He discovers the fox isn't after him anymore.
He rests,
then surrounded by mystery,
rabbit disappears into the night

Elizabeth Oliver :: Grade 4
Royal Oaks Elementary School :: Woodbury

NIGHT POEM

At night
the moon sings to me.
At night
the stars play cards with me.
At night
the sky gives me food sometimes
At night
I hear the crickets and they always have a party with me
At night
when it rains, I fall asleep

Anna Hutchinson :: Grade 2
Highland Elementary School :: St. Paul

Night is like darkness
and coke
like when the fire wood
is all burnt
or black, black chocolate
or when the sky is really black
or if the lake is really deep
the water is kind of black
or a black
costume the witches wear
or like black paint
or the chalkboard
or black shoes
When it's night time
I hold my pillow
and bed. They
protect me
from shadows.

Melissa Sarles :: Grade 3
Shirley Hills Elementary School :: Mound

When the sun goes into its hole in the earth for
a night's hibernation, my mystic brother sets away.

He opens his magical book to the page he
wants and then he steps in.

I look in the book and watch him do
the magical things he does.

He races the golden eagle.

He hunts with the two headed wolves.

He talks to the king of dreams.

Then the sun wakes up, he jumps out, and
we go to school.

Christian Maire :: Grade 5
Gatewood Elementary School :: Hopkins

I Saw the Sun

The moon crossed the sun after lunch.
My teacher (the one with the bobbed brown hair
who put on lipstick during handwriting class)
kept us inside.
"Eclipses hurt young eyes."

I sat on the wet beach, a mat of moss beside me.
My newspaper bags hung from my ten-speed,
my headphones rested in my lap.
The houses across the lake woke up one at a time
(blinded by kitchen lights in the dark)
the lake in front of me was as flat
as a parking lot, until a mallard broke into flight
announcing the sun
rising over the new apartments
like a nite-lite in the hallway.

As a child, I would stare into the sun
until I couldn't see my younger sister.

The first being
the first organism
the first earthen animal, my earliest ancestor
that developed eyes
stared up through the ocean,
saw the sun,
and was blinded.

Dan Marshall :: Grade 12
Osseo High School :: Osseo

RAINING

I pull the soft covers to my chin and curl up
like the small, fluffy kitten at the end of my bed.
The droplets of rain explode on the barrier window
like tiny water balloons trying to break in.
The constant pounding of the rain
competes with the kitten's loud purring.
Thunder clashes from the sky and I jump.
     Everything is silent. Then,
         plip, plip, plip,
the rain continues, neverending, like the wind.

Upstairs, footsteps are heading for the kitchen.
They will soon fall back into slumber
and I will lie awake, listening intensely,
to what the rain may have to say.

Trisha Garness :: Grade 8
Shakopee Junior High School :: Shakopee

Dear Tornado,

You scare me and blow things around. I have no place to go when you attack me. Stay away from me. You get me in the house at night when I am asleep. I get scared seeing you panic when I see you out the window. I can't go anywhere cause you go so fast and I can't catch up with you. You can blow my house away and kill me. I don't like you. You are nasty to me all the time. You form from the sky and spin. And it is neat when I see you spin. You go so fast that a car can't catch up with you. You are the fastest on earth. Please stay away from me. I can stay in the house. In the basement. The end.

Mark Watrin :: Grade 3
Sandstone Elementary School :: Sandstone

Hey kid! Watch that old man's hat.
Keep in touch, old woman, with
        your umbrella.
See the child with his homework
        papers?
I'm the wind called wild.

See the bird so slight in flight?
Hear the leaves dancing?
Feel a chill go down your back?
Yes, I'm the wind called soft.

Watch those waters form those caps.
Hear the trees creak.
Watch the blackened clouds roll in.
I'm the wind called storm.

Prudence Lind :: Grade 11
Rush City Schools :: Rush City

The wind wears a tuxedo to the
tornado prom. He tastes like toothpaste
and he looks like a flying saucer and he feels
like a pillow. He sounds like someone whistling.
He plays on my swingset and lives under
rocks. He dreams of superman and pie.
He talks to the sun.

Steven Watson :: Grade 2
Birch Lake Elementary School :: White Bear Lake

Goldenrod:
Tall and resolute, standing firm among society's
Solid brown earth base.
Yellow flower of setting sun, end of day's labor, blooming
Realist. Flower of setting suns.

Daffodil, narcissus — Greek mythology,
Gentle and smooth youth; childhood visionary,
Unrequited love, trust in the
Yellow flower of glistening dew; tears of punishment,
Idealist.

Rose:
Crystal smile with thorns, conceit, opinion;
Supporting lattice. Officious
Yellow flower of shrinking stars.
Pragmatist, shielding and burying compassion.

Daisy: she loves me; she loves me not;
Tinted with striate proportions,
Separating whole — analyzing parts.
Yellow flower of drying cloud;
Analyst.

Buttercup:
Lobed fingers; small offering, many
Blended soils surround. Held as one, compromise of all.
Yellow flower of blinking moon. Cause and effect; moon and
    tide;
Synthesis.

Karen Sherper :: Grade 10
Elk River Senior High School :: Elk River

FLOWER ODE

Ye daffodils so beautiful,
petals so delicate,
you look like scrambled eggs
lying on the ground.
Blessed are the roses
and the marigolds,
magnificent balls of fire,
yet not harmful to anyone.
The violet is a blot of paint
left by an artist's palette,
Spreading peace and beauty
all across the land.
Flowers make that joy and beauty.
Winter is cruel,
freezing them in ice.
But utmost joy is when
spring comes
and the first flower blooms.

Group Poem :: Grades 5 & 6
Franklin Elementary School :: Mankato

THE RED ROSE
(FROM PAINTINGS BY RENE MAGRITTE)

Look at the blood red rose.
It makes the lives of all
men fall from the sky.
It makes all mirrors turn away
It makes the empty door
full and cheerful.
It makes the window
reflect and makes
the castle rise
and finds the feet of a body
and lets the doves
escape in peace.
That's what the red rose does.

Brandi Ludlow :: Grade 5
West Concord Elementary School :: West Concord

The four deer stand there in the
melting snow waiting for
the buds. No canopy to hide under,
the lifeless forest awaits the praise of
the green. They are
statues standing there with clocks
inside themselves, awaiting
the green, killing the baby
aspens until the green comes.
The bark is getting smaller, awaiting the
green, the dwindling bark.

Erik Fluegel :: Grade 8
Mounds Park Academy :: St. Paul

ME, THE TREE
(FOR ARBOR DAY)

Me, the tree, King of the Jungle
with my branches reaching the sky,
Always producing life for mankind
with the wind combing through my branches,
never disagreeing with my work.

Brett Phillips :: Grade 5
Elm Creek Elementary School :: Maple Grove

Until last weekend, I never noticed something in the treehouse in the woods. The trees and the animals started to talk to each other. I just sat there to see what they were saying, but just then, they noticed me and stopped talking. The animals stopped and everything was so quiet! I went up and talked to the trees. They were very shy. I asked why they didn't like humans? No answer, until one of the trees started to say, "I hate humans because they pound nails into us!"

I replied, "I pounded the nails into you to build my treehouse." Everything was quiet, a few minutes passed, the ground started to shake! The clouds grew black and heavy! The sun was playing hide and seek with the earth. I wished I wasn't there! Another second passed, the vines of the tree started to clasp my feet! I tried to run away but I tripped on the vines! The birds started to shriek at me! It sounded like a Skil saw! I couldn't think! I shouted, "Quiet!"

I asked the birds, "What's the matter now?"

"You stole our nests!"

"But I had to! For science class!" My backyard was like a jungle, all vines and shrieking birds! I felt like I was in the Amazon. It was horrible! The vines of all the trees started to come up to form a cage around me! The birds started to turn into parrots and vultures and Pterodons! Everything stopped for about two minutes, the ground started to grow and formed a bench around a redwood tree. There was a jury which was made out of 3 birch trees, 4 Pterodons, 3 oak trees and 2 parrots. The bailiff was a tree with a thermometer on it that looked like a mean ugly face! My tree house turned into a two story building. "I wonder why they still have this cage around me," I said aloud.

"I know why they still have you in this cage."

"Who said that?"

"Me."

"Well, then who's me?"

"I am. The only thing in the backyard of yours that likes you! I'm a termite."

"You don't even know me. Why do you like me?"

"Because when you made your tree house you left wood chips behind! Yum! I'm sitting in your side pocket."

"Say Mr. Termite. If you like me, then would you be my lawyer?"

"Sure. But I need a tape recorder and microphone."

"Chew me out of this cage, and if I win, I'll give you an expensive piece of wood for your troubles."

"You have a deal!"

We walked into the courtroom and . . .

(to be continued)

Jason Tyge :: Grade 5
Rossman Elementary School :: Detroit Lakes

THE FOREST

The forest
is
green
the sky
is blue
When I
get to
the forest
the first thing I do
is put my tent up
get my play clothes on
then look for a stick
sharpen it find
a hiding
place and wait till
it's dark then
I turn on my flashlight
and run around
look for
blue trees and
yellow leaves
or pink grass a
gray moon
and red and green
rocks
but I
never
could seem
to find
them

but every
time I go there I look
look and look

Amber Schmitz :: Grade 4
John F. Kennedy Elementary School :: Hastings

SPRING

Open the door to the bright sun.
Wake up the velvet rose and the silk tulips.
Invite the gold canary
and big bear.
We are having a party
at the shining river.

Eric Buringrud :: Grade 2
Lakeview Elementary School :: Robbinsdale

A piece of gold
In the coal of life
soft as the down of a swan
Comfort me as I pause
Whisper to me in the wind
The song of flying free

Wes Taylor :: Grade 7
Fred Moore Junior High School :: Anoka

THE WORLD

Someday I am going to all the atomic bases
and deconstruct atomic bombs and replace them with artificial
ones.
Someday I am going to invent a machine that could survive
1200° Fahrenheit
and travel to the center of the earth
and float around awhile.
Someday I will go flying in a Boeing 747 and parachute
up and up into outer space.
Someday I want my mom to buy more sugar cereals.
Someday I am going from New York to Morocco and then to
Syria and then to Italy, and then fly to Sydney, Australia, and
then to Lima, Peru, and back home in five months.
Someday, accidentally, I am going to discover
a new set of planets revolving around a different star.
Someday I am going to wake up and discover
chocolate has vitamins A, B, C, B-12, C-16 and A-14.
Someday I will be sitting in my laboratory-to-be
and I will discover a definite cure for AIDS.
Someday the USSR and the USA will cut out all troopers
and deconstruct all forms of defense.

Jesse Berezovsky :: Grade 3
Meadowbrook Elementary School :: Golden Valley

Each and every time I smell gasoline, snowmobile gasoline to be exact, it takes me back to 1982. I am 4 years old, it is bitterly cold, -22 degrees. My father is helping me put on my snowsuit. First my long under clothes, then my gloves come, layer after layer like a bed with 100 sheets. Then my hood, my facemask, my hat. Then my boots, I lace them up to almost my knee and tie them almost air tight to my foot. We go outside — the cold chill of mother nature rips and tears at me. Suddenly I hear a noise and the smell of gas fills my head. We weave and wind our way through the forest. It seems like a dream, trying to find our home with the sound of a motor and the smell of gas filling my head with pictures of a warm imaginary cabin in the woods.

Mark Sundrud :: Grade 5
Northern Elementary School :: Bemidji

DACHAU

Every time I hear the name Munich I get the shivers. The reason is the time I was there.

It's July of 1988. My birthday is the 19th. My father is a professor and he has to go overseas to a place near Hitler's Eagle's Nest, which I've found out is only a mile away from where we're staying right now. In fact, I can see it right from our window. Anyway, he's here for a new program called overseas DoDDS, a military school for kids of military families in the US Army.

Today we are going up to Munich. I think this will be exciting, but my parents seem kind of gloomy about going. When we get to Munich we go to a suburb called Dachau. I realize what it is and remember hearing my parents telling me about this on the airplane. One of Hitler's death camps during WWII.

We go inside and the first thing I see is this black wall which reminds me of the Vietnam Memorial. It has the names of certain countries and under each, the numbers of how many people died from that nation.

When we walk past that wall, we see a museum-like showcase. The one picture that makes me hate the city most is of a scientist who had taken a brain out of a person who was still alive. The scientist was smiling like he didn't care about what he was doing.

After that we went to a movie theater-like place. It says on the door, in four different languages, "No kids under 12." My parents let me in anyway because they figure I can handle the movie. It is live footage of the concentration camps dubbed in English. It shows how they put dozens of dead people who probably starved to death into a train with wheelbarrows. The people who were pulling the wagons wore masks to filter the air. The majority of the people had died in the gas chambers of the Nazi camp in Auschwitz. The movies also showed how Hitler came to power.

After that I had nightmares for weeks, and occasionally sick and gruesome daydreams. But I don't think I'll ever forget the holocaust.

Jim Austad :: Grade 5
Northern Elementary School :: Bemidji

MY FATHER

My father is the dream caster
casting my dreams along the moonlit sky.
He is like a wizard and knows things about me
only I should know.
He sets me free among graceful seagulls.
He's turned my life into a field of galloping stallions
and takes all the pressure away when I'm with him.
He patches up all the holes in my life.
How? How can he manage all of that?

Alexandra Person :: Grade 5
Alice Smith Elementary School :: Hopkins

WINDOW POEM

When I look outside I see
    old white haired people
    coming out doors to steep stairs
    Sholom Home peace signs posted
    in moist snow-filled ground
    dark red lights on an ambulance
    hurrying down the street
Then I look away

Rykken Young :: Grade 6
Chelsea Heights Elementary School :: St. Paul

Have you ever thought about
old rusty cars with no tires?
Have you ever thought about
old weed-covered football fields?
Have you ever thought about
old melted color crayons without an owner?
Have you ever thought about
an old worn out house without a buyer?
Have you ever thought about
old trees that are falling down?
Have you ever thought about
old fields without crops?
Have you ever thought about
lonely stray dogs?
Have you ever thought about
music without notes?
Have you ever thought about old
cracked dishes without food on them?
Have you ever thought about old gardens
overgrown with weeds?
Have you ever thought about all the things
there are to think about?

Andy Lenartz :: Grade 5
Pine Hill Elementary School :: Cottage Grove

FOG

Mist.
Cloudy.
Thick.
It's like pea soup.
Headlights with no cars.
Little eyeballs shining.
Can't see.
Like a white snowstorm.
Where's my next step
    going to be?
Like driving through a grey wall.
Scary.
Nothing in sight.
Thousands and millions of white ghosts.
Travelling through my mother's grey makeup.
Going through a dirty bathtub.
The sun is lost.
When is it going to end?
Fog.

Group Poem :: Grade 5
Woodbury Junior High School :: Woodbury

My block is safe.
There are nice people and mean people
but not many kids on my
block, mostly teenagers.
They are tall and skinny.
I'm short and skinny.
My house is a blue rambler.
No pool, no hot tub.
My dog's dad, Jock, lived 17 years.
What a dog.
This is how
I am going to live.

Carrie Ann Borle :: Grade 2
Wyoming Elementary School :: Wyoming

He'd never really thought about it, maybe because he wasn't the type and he wasn't really into stuff like that but it all happened kinda fast, somewhat like a daring roller coaster ride, scary and thrilling and incredibly quick which later he translated into a trip and actually, he might not have done it at all but one night when he was out with the boys at a really smokin' party he found himself huddled deep in a corner where the laughter and noise of the party didn't reach and the guys spoke in quiet, almost reverent tones which awed him for they seemed to respect this fine, silky powder stretched out in slender lines on the oak table and one by one they took turns, one smooth sniff and he watched in utter fascination as it disappeared into their faces and then the calm before the onslaught of emotions and visions they had and Rex (yeah, that was this guy's real name) would smile maliciously and say, "Man, what a rush," which made him feel like a member of an exclusive club so it came to his turn and he was a little uncertain until they all stared at him with deep, wicked smiles and he told himself, what the hell, and breathed it in slow — and suddenly his thoughts spun and whirled themselves into useless fragments and poorly developed photographs and for some odd reason he thought of the night he went swimming — no clothes on — in Lisa Hamilton's pool while she and Jeff made out in the trees and then these illusions thinned out and slipped from his head and a calm, woozy calm, settled in and he casually leaned back and breathed, "Man, what a rush," and Rex, looking evil, clapped him with a dead hand on the shoulder, shook him a little and grinned, "Yo, bro," well, then, after that he had no conscience and did coke whenever convenient, at school, between classes, at the apartment or parties (though never at work — hell, *he* wasn't stupid) but little by little all else dropped from his life, even Lisa, bewildered and angered by his nonchalance and violent temper and he, well he just drifted further and further away in his world of substance until gradually every day faded and blurred with the edges of the next and he felt like a sick, empty man . . . .

And he left, without much of a mark on this world, just another statistic on the annual report . . . another cocaine addict.

Keli Larson :: Grade 12
John Marshall Senior High School :: Rochester

When I was one I was Mommy's Little Baker.
When I was two I was Frightened Leave Me Alone.
When I was three I was My Brother's Best Friend.
When I was four I was Little Miss Curious.
When I was five I was Monkey See-Monkey Do.
When I was six I was The Bright Light Bulb Girl.
When I was seven I was Little Miss Ask Them All.
When I was eight I was Miss Pretty Lace and Frills.
When I was nine I was Act It Out.
Now I'm ten and I'm Miss Mixed Up.

Sonja Kjellberg :: Grade 5
Glen Lake Elementary School :: Minnetonka

Owl, Wise, Owl, up in a tree,
please will you come with me?
We will find mice for you
and apples and cookies for me.
Will you teach me how to fly?

Owl, Owl, come with me.
We will find a rope.
Owl, fly after the rope and bite it.
Owl, we will go play tug of war.

We will play hide and go seek.
Will you teach me how to make a nest?
Do you fly south in the winter?
How do you get up in your tree
and don't fall?
How do you get your food?

Group Poem :: Grade 1
Webster Magnet School :: St. Paul